12/2/9⁴

Dear Sharon

With love

fro Sharon Jameja

Yorkshire Terriers

Dedication

This book is dedicated to my family and many friends, including Yorkies, who have helped me set off on my happy adventures with the breed. The breeding and showing through the years have given me memories that will last a lifetime. I should also like to pay a special tribute to the breeders of long ago who helped to make the Yorkshire Terrier what it is today.

YORKSHIRE TERRIERS

AN OWNER'S COMPANION

Osman Sameja

The Crowood Press

First published in 1992 by
The Crowood Press Ltd
Ramsbury, Marlborough
Wiltshire SN8 2HR

British Library Cataloguing in Publication Data

A catalogue record for this book is available
from the British Library.

ISBN 1 85223 529 2

Throughout this book, 'he' has been used as a neutral pronoun,
and is intended to refer to both sexes.

Typeset by Inforum Typesetting, Portsmouth
Printed and bound in Great Britain by
BPCC Hazell Books, Aylesbury

Contents

Foreword

Reading this book by Osman Sameja has given me immense pleasure. I believe that this publication will prove to be irresistible reading to all who have an interest in the Yorkshire Terrier, and I am sure that they will find each chapter as factual, informative and interesting as I have.

Those owners, or prospective owners, of this most endearing of breeds, who may be contemplating a move into the fascinating and rewarding world of breeding and showing, will find these pages packed with invaluable information and useful tips on these specialist fields. Included are chapters dedicated to such arts as the growing and preparation of the Yorkie's coat for the show ring.

Those readers who have a more general interest are also well catered for in the sections which explore the history of the Yorkshire Terrier as a breed; from its creation, through its establishment as a breed in its own right and up to the present date. There are many wonderful photographs and illustrations, both historical and modern.

In my opinion no one could have written such a book with more authority than Osman Sameja. His British champions hold all records with twelve champion males in direct line and five champion females in direct line. In all, the Ozmilion champions have sired more champions than any other Yorkshire Terrier kennels in Great Britain, and the crowning glory of this success story must be Osman's male Champion Ozmilion Dedication who is the top-winning Yorkshire Terrier with fifty-two Challenge Certificates.

Joyce W. Mann
International All-Rounder judge and
owner of Craigsbank Yorkshire Terrier

Preface

This book has been written to help new owners and breeders to understand Yorkshire Terriers, the breed we know as 'Yorkies'. It is hoped that it will give an idea of their history and origins and some ideas of what to look for in the new puppy, the brood-bitch, the stud-dog and the show dog. It is also an opportunity to record our thanks to the breeders of earlier years whose efforts have given us the most popular toy dog in the world today. This breed of little dog has captured the hearts of hundreds of thousands of people and given countless hours of pleasure and devoted loyalty to their owners. Even in advanced old age, Yorkies can still run and play almost as if they were puppies.

The endless fascination of trying to breed the super specimen that will take on all comers in the show ring is both a delight and a challenge, but whatever their size, shape or colour, Yorkies are usually a constant pleasure to own and good company for young or old alike. If they are not, it is usually the owner's fault for forgetting that, as puppies, they are still little terriers, not toys, and that they are very intelligent dogs who do need proper training if they are to thrive in a family environment.

I should like to express my sincere thanks to all those who have assisted me in the preparation of this book.

For their wonderful photographs I am indebted to Barbara and Bill Burrows of Thomas Fall; also to Arthur Brownscombe and Marc Henrie for the cover photographs. Thanks to the family of the late George Tomkins and his late daughter Elsie Tomkins for the use of their collection of old photographs.

For their help, loyalty and support, I am grateful to my dear friends Madelaine Guarnière, Paul Clarke, Margaret Carey, Richard Haynes, Jeanette Haynes, Joe Magri, Steve Marshall, Liz Putman, and very special thanks to Mary Jones without whom this would not have been possible.

Finally, I must record my thanks to the Yorkshire Terriers, past and present, who have given me so much pleasure and heart-break and so many successes at the highest level in the British show ring and have been such a part of my life for more than three decades.

Osman Sameja 1991

1

History of the Breed

Origins

The ancestors of the Yorkshire Terrier were most certainly working dogs and known as terriers of one type or another. These working dogs would be used by hunters in search of prey such as rabbits and also to keep down vermin such as rats.

The name terrier comes from the Latin *terra*, which means earth; so these short-legged dogs who would scour the earth in search of their prey. Although their long rough coats would get very messy, this would not have been considered a problem in most households of the time. In fact the long coat was ideal for these little hunting dogs, as it could be used to pull them out of holes and ditches they had entered in the course of their hunting. It was from this type of early terrier that the Yorkshire Terrier descended.

In the 1990s, the exact origins of the Yorkshire Terrier are very much shrouded in the mists of time. I think some present-day writers are very brave, if not even foolish, to make strong statements as to the exact ancestors of the breed we know today. I prefer to go back to the knowledgeable writers of years gone by, who were at least a little closer in time to those original breeders.

Take, for instance, Rawdon B. Lee, the former editor of *The Field*: in his *Modern Dogs*, published by Horace Cox in 1896, he refers to Yorkshire and other terriers. He writes:

> The charming aristocratic little dog we now know as the Yorkshire terrier has been identified as such for a comparatively short period, the Kennel Club adopting this nomenclature in their Stud Book for 1886, although many of them are still registered under the head of Toy terriers (rough).

Prior to this date the name had been hanging about him for some few years, because the titles of rough, broken-haired, or Scotch terrier, under which he was first known, were most misleading. During the early days of dog shows the classes in which he competed included terriers of almost any variety, from cross-bred mongrel to the Dandie Dinmont, the Skye Terrier and the Bedlington.

Unfortunately for us, early records are very vague as to how the Yorkshire Terrier as we now know him came into being. Throughout his history many commentators have put forward different theories on the combinations that make up his ancestry. These have included the Clydesdale Terrier or Paisley Terrier, the Black and Tan English Toy Terrier and the Maltese Terrier in varying degrees. Rawdon Lee offers us one possible explanation:

> How the name 'Scotch terrier' became attached to a dog which so thoroughly had its home in Yorkshire and Lancashire is somewhat difficult to determine, if it can be determined at all, but a very old breeder of the variety told me that the first of them originally came from Scotland, where they had been accidentally produced from a cross between the silky coated Skye terrier (the Clydesdale) and the black and tan terrier. One could scarcely expect that a pretty dog, taking in some degree after both its parents, could be produced from a first cross between a smooth-coated dog and a long-coated bitch or vice versa. Maybe two or three animals so bred had been brought by some weavers into Yorkshire, and there suitably admired, pains were taken to perpetuate the strain.
>
> There appears to be something feasible and practical in this story, and I am sorry that when this information was given to me nearly a quarter of a century ago by a Yorkshire weaver, then sixty years old and since dead, I did not obtain more particulars about what was in the day called the 'Scotch terrier'.

Whatever his parentage, this terrier had good breeding and the development of his superb long coat helped to transform him from a hard-working dog to a much admired breed sought after for his looks and personality. It was during the mid-nineteenth century that the first dog shows were held in England and greater thought was given to breeding and Breed Standards. This increase in interest in showing dogs was certainly beneficial in the development of the Yorkshire Terrier as we know him.

It was in the 1870s that this 'rough-haired Scotch terrier' became known as the Yorkshire Terrier, probably because the breed had been so improved with examples bred in the north of England, and Yorkshire in particular. Now, almost one hundred years since his writing, Mr Lees' next comments make interesting reading:

Mr and Mrs Greenwood's Ch. Pellon Little Benjamin.

However, this is the Yorkshire terrier now, and will no doubt remain so till the end of his time or until his place, usurped by other dogs which certainly not handsomer, will be less difficult to keep in prime coat and in good condition.

Fortunately, the difficulty of looking after the Yorkshire Terrier's coat has not deterred breeders and owners from this superb breed of dog, and the Yorkshire Terrier is far from being usurped by other dogs. The popularity of the breed in these early days is confirmed by Mr Lee as he writes about one of the early fanciers, Peter Eden of Manchester:

... in its [the Yorkshire Terrier's] early days he owned some very excellent specimens which for the most part he purchased from the working men in Lancashire. It was they who bred them and delighted to show them at the local exhibitions, of which that at Middleton, near Manchester was the chief. Here, and at the Belle Vue shows, were

11

Violet Ellicott, Edwardian stage actress with her tiny Yorkie.

always to be found the choicest specimens, which their owners trea-sured with great care, who had to be uncommonly hard up to be induced to sell their favourites. They would get £20 or £30 for a good specimen, more if it was extra special. And this at a time when dogs did not run to [as] much money as they do now. We have on record that Mrs Troughear of Leeds sold her little dog Conqueror to Mrs Emmott, wife of an American actor for £250.

Considering it was the late 1800s these prices were very high for any dog, and so testify to the desirability and growing popularity of this new breed. This early breed was somewhat different to the Breed Standard we look to today. As there was no Breed Standard in the very early days there was great variance in the examples entered at shows. As the breed developed though, it quickly moved towards creating a Standard, and one aspect of this was the general size of the Yorkshire Terrier, who became smaller as he moved towards the twentieth century. This is confirmed by Mr Lee who in 1896 wrote:

Miss Gladys Kurion and her little Yorkie.

'Originally this terrier was a bigger dog than he is today, specimens from 10lb in weight to 14lb being not at all uncommon, so repeatedly classes had to be provided for them in two sections – dogs over 8lb and dogs under that weight – whilst in addition there might be divisions for rough haired toy terriers, the maximum allowed being 6lb'. At the time I write, Yorkshire terriers over 8lb weight are seldom seen at our canine gatherings, the prevailing weight being, I should say, from 4lb to 6lb. But the club scales still allow for two classes, their restrictions being 12lb maximum in the one and 5lb in the other.

We learn from Mr Lee's writings that it was the Yorkshires' coats that were most influential in their rise as pets and as show dogs. He writes:

'The Yorkshire Terrier at his best is a smart, handsome little dog and some I have known to be handy rat killers, although, as a rule they were kept as pets and for show purposes. If running outside on a wet day or dirty day, their beautiful long silky coats get bedraggled, some-times almost spoiled and ruined, even in the house extraordinary care

Mr and Mrs Greenwood's Ch. Wee Pellon Eclipse, son of Ch. Star of Pellon.

must be taken to keep the coat of the Yorkshire Terrier in order. Indeed it has been said that the number of exhibitors in this country who thoroughly understand the treatment of this little pet dog can be counted on the fingers of two hands. Whether this is so or not, I will not commit myself by saying, but I do know that a 'Yorkshire' shown by someone who 'knows how' and by someone who does 'not know how' are terribly different in appearance. Indeed the extraordinary growth of the coat to be found on a perfect specimen is in a certain degree due to artificial aid, for when comparatively young the skin at the roots of the hair is dressed daily with an ointment or wash which acts in a wonderful manner in stimulating the growth of the hair.

These early well-groomed examples of the breed certainly did much to glamorize the breed and so contribute to its increasing popularity. Beside so much time and work being put into the coats, other areas of the dog's appearance were considered for potential improvement. Rawdon Lee goes on to say that,

Yorkshire Terriers, once upon a time, had as a rule his ears cut, but

Mable Love, another Edwardian actress with her much-loved pet.

Myriam Clement, holding her pet Yorkie.

15

The founding father of the Yorkshire Terrier, Mrs J. Foster's
Huddersfield Ben 1865–71.

now this mutilation is since discontinued, we shall find him with neat drop ears he often carried at the earlier shows where classes were provided. Peter Eden's Albert, a particularly good dog in his day, had natural drop ears. The practice of cropping this little dog was absolutely useless from any point of view, for whilst the mutilation might have given a perkiness and smartness to a short coated dog, the length of the jacket on a good specimen Yorkshire terrier almost entirely covered the ears.

With the increasing popularity of showing dogs, more and more aspects of the dog's characteristics were noted, and records kept. The growing interest in the dog and his development led to the founding of the Kennel Club in Great Britain in 1873 and the establishment of individual breeds. Importance was placed on parentage, and so

Pedigree of Huddersfield Ben

Parents	Grand Parents	Great Grand Parents	Great Great Grand Parents
Sire Mr Bascovitch's Dog	Ramsden's Bounce	Ramsden's Bob	Haigh's Teddy Old Dolly
		Old Dolly	Albert
	Eastwood's Lady	Eastwood's Old Ben	Ramsden's Old Ben Young Dolly
		Young Dolly	Old Sandy Old Dolly
Dam Eastwood's Lady	Eastwood's Old Ben	Ramsden's Bounce	Ramsden's Bob Old Dolly
		Young Dolly	Old Sandy Old Sally
	Young Dolly	Old Sandy	Haigh's Teddy Kitty
		Old Dolly	Albert

pedigrees were documented that now help us in determining the progress towards a Breed Standard for Yorkshire Terriers.

It is because of this documenting that we know the pedigree of Huddersfield Ben, who was probably one of the most famous early examples of the breed and was bred by Mr W. Eastwood in 1865. Huddersfield Ben was brought and successfully shown by Mrs Jonas Foster of Bradford, a lady who played a leading role in promoting the Yorkshire Terrier in his early days. Despite his untimely death and short life – just six and a half years – Huddersfield Ben had been referred to as the 'Father of Yorkshire Terriers' and was sire to many fine offspring, so helping to shape this early breed. He and many others are rated as contributing to the early days of the breed and Mr Lee charmingly pays tribute to these famous dogs and breeders.

Past Successes Count

Actual measurements do not count for very much, but the length of hair on the body and head of some of the best dogs is almost

The author's Ch. Ozmilion Dedication, the top-winning Yorkshire Terrier of all time (1989).

incredible, and its texture and colour extraordinary. It is said that when in his best form the little dog Conqueror, already alluded to, had hair of an almost uniform length of 24 inches (60cm) and weighed in at about 5½ pounds (2.5kg). One of the smartest little dogs of the variety, and a game little chap too, was Mr T. Kirby's Smart, who did a lot of winning over twenty years ago. Old Huddersfield was another of the pillars of the breed, Mrs Troughear's Dreadnought was likewise a celebrity, and Mrs Foster's (Bradford) Bright and Sandy were notable dogs a few years ago. Indeed, to the latter (one of the few lady judges) and to her husband Jonas Foster, more than to anyone else is due much of the popularity the Yorkshire Terrier possesses today. They have bred them for years and have from time to time owned the most perfect specimens imaginable. Mrs Foster's Ted, who weighed 5 pounds (2.3kg), has perhaps never been bettered for all-round excellence, and it was extremely funny to see this mite of a dog competing against an enormous St Bernard or dignified Bloodhound for the cup for the best animal in show. Nor did the award always go to the big and strong. One of the tiniest dogs I ever saw was a Yorkshire Terrier Mrs Foster showed at Westminster Aquarium in 1893. Mite by name and by nature, she weighed only a couple of pounds and was nicely formed, of fair colour and quite active, even more so than some of the larger breeds.

Mrs Foster has also owned other diminutive but perky little creatures: Bradford Marie, who weighed, when fully mature, only 31 ounces (8.7g) and Bradford Queen of the Toys whose weight is but 24 ounces. Yet both are or were quite active and thoroughly well built. Another extraordinary Yorkshire was Mrs Vaughan Fowler's Longbridge Bat, who weighed 2¾ pounds (1.25kg) and is particularly smart and lively. Mrs Walton and Mrs Beard of Ashton-under-Lyne had taken high positions as breeders of Yorkshire Terriers and their Ashton King, Queen and Ashton Bright are certainly three of the best specimens of the day. Bradford Ben, Bradford Venus and Bradford Mabel, first shown by Mrs Foster, are likewise quite tiptop, whilst Mrs Vaughan Fowler's Longbridge Bob and Daisy and Bradford Marie already alluded to, are or were in the front rank. Unfortunately the last named died before she had quite reached her best. Another good Yorkshire was Mrs Smith's Nancy's Sister; and Mrs White, a lady residing in Scotland, was the owner of two or three specimens above the average, including Bradford Dickens and Grindlay Hero.

The best of the variety are certainly kept in very few hands. Amongst the old breeders were also Mr John Inman of Brighouse; Mr Abe Boulton, Accrington; Mrs Alderson, Leeds; Mr Cavanagh, Leeds; Mr Greenwood, Bradford; Mrs Bligh Monck, Reading; Lady Giffard, Redhill and Mr Wilkinson, Halifax. The best modern kennels of the day were those of Mrs Foster at Bradford; Mrs Vaughan Fowler,

Jack Wood's Ch. Armley Governor.

19

Longbridge Warwick; Mr J.B. Leech, Clifton Bristol; Mr T.D. Hodgson, Halifax; Mrs Walton and Mrs Beard, Ashton-under-Lyne; Mrs Farquhar, Paisley; and Mrs R. White, Edinburgh.

The Yorkshire Terrier was by no means a common commodity and although third- and fourth-rate specimens could be purchased from London dealers, Bradford was their home. There it was not difficult to obtain a suitable dog at a fair price. It is said that upon one occasion the late Mr E. Sandell required three or four for a certain purpose and was unable to obtain one from London so he took a journey to Bradford or Halifax, I quite forget which, and there he made public his intention to give a prize of a sovereign or two for the best York-

In Edinburgh, Mary Lowrie with her aunt and uncle and the Lilyhill Yorkies (1930s).

shire Terrier to be exhibited at a public house on a certain evening. As additional inducement, no entry fee was required. In due course, an excellent collection of Yorkshire Terriers was brought together, from which the enterprising promoter speedily selected and purchased what he required.

Unfortunately we will never really know what ingredients were used by the early breeder in forming the Yorkshire Terrier, but the top-winning Yorkshire Terrier of all time, Ch. Ozmilion Dedication, is exactly twenty-nine generations on his extended pedigree from Mrs Foster's famous Huddersfield Ben, through Ozmilion, Beechrise and Pagnell, to the Invincias that directly descended from Mrs Foster's stock.

A great deal of thanks must be given to this lady who has done so much in the past to make the Yorkshire what it is today. Her name has appeared for over fifty years and we know she travelled the length and breadth of the country showing her dogs. This is remarkable bearing in mind that travel in those days was far more arduous than it is today. She had the honour to become the first lady to judge the toy breeds and her ability to produce champion after champion under her Bradford affix proved her quite capable.

Inspired by the interest shown, the Yorkshire Terrier Club was formed in 1898 and the committee drew up the Breed Standard which remained unaltered until 1987. The evolution of the Yorkshire Terrier from obscure and humble beginnings is a phenomenal feat for any breed; clubs and societies now exist all over the world, as far apart as Belgium, South America and Japan.

Twentieth-Century Kennels

Although the Yorkshire Terrier was quickly becoming a sought-after dog both as a fashion accessory and as a show dog, the actual number of Yorkshire Terriers living at the turn of the century was very small in comparison with the vast number living today. Much of the credit for their increasing success as a breed must go to the dogs themselves. Their character, looks and practicability have made them firm favourites with successive generations of dog owners. As well as the dogs themselves getting the glory, much credit must also go to the many fine breeders who, through their dedication and tremendous efforts, have ensured the Yorkshire Terrier's position as one of the most successful dogs of the twentieth century.

Mary Lowrie with Ch. Lilyhill Spider in 1920.

One way to judge the growth of the breed is to study the number of registrations at the Kennel Club. In 1894, there were just twenty-four Yorkshire Terriers registered with the Kennel Club. This number increased gradually over the years and during the 1930s the number fluctuated between 200 and 300 registrations. It was not until after the Second World War that the registrations increased sharply and phenomenal interest in the breed began.

In 1945, there were 479 Yorkshire Terriers registered; by 1960, this had risen to 3,863 and, by 1969, the registrations topped 10,000 for the first time. Five years later 15,147 were registered at the Kennel Club and Yorkshire Terriers became the most registered breed in the UK. Although this reflects the breed's great growth rate, it is the famous dogs and their breeders who tell the real story of the Yorkshire Terrier's fabulous success during the twentieth century.

Ch. Harringay Remarkable, winner of 9 CCs and many times the Best Toy in Show. Breeder and owner Mr and Mrs E.H. Clenshaw.

The First Forty Years

With the formation of the Yorkshire Terrier Club in 1898, the Yorkshire Terrier was well set to enter the twentieth century. From the excellent breeding of a number of dedicated breeders, the Breed Standard was drawn up and accepted and became the goal of all Yorkshire Terrier breeders.

It was still some time before dog showing was popular enough for the breed to be given classes of its own. Travelling to dog shows up and down the country was no easy feat and so the number of Yorkshire Terriers entered at any particular show was limited. This meant that they had to compete against other breeds for their titles and prizes, their competition being other toy and broken-haired terriers. Because of this the number of Yorkshire Terriers gaining championship status was small when compared with the post-war period.

Not all breeders were interested in showing the dogs and so it was left to dog fanciers to bring their dogs to the show ring. Partly because of this and partly because few kennels registered a prefix, the process of tracing some dogs' ancestry can be difficult. Fortunately, there have been a number of breeders who have had a long association with the breed and can provide complete records of their dogs.

Mary Lowrie with her Lilyhill Superb (1940s).

One such breeder was George Tomkins, who started his kennel during the last century. They continued within his family right up until 1979 when his Charleview kennel was disbanded following the death of his daughter Elsie Tomkins. In the early days, Mr Tomkins had three particularly notable dogs: Little Impertenance, Duros Perfection and Armley Tiny Fritz who was bred by Jack Wood. Many of the Charleview dogs can be traced back to Mrs Foster's stock.

Sprig of Blossom was a well-known winner during the second decade of this century. She is credited with twenty-six CCs (Championship Certificates), both her parents were unregistered and she was bred by Mr W. Wood. Sprig of Blossom was shown and made famous by her second owners Mr and Mrs Dick Marshall, who had a long association with the breed and owned many champions.

Mrs Annie Swan began her long association with Yorkshire Terriers during the 1920s and bred a number of champions throughout her career. She has been a major influence in the breed. Prior to the Second World War, she had bred some excellent Yorkshire Terriers, many of whom could trace their line back to Halifax Marvel, a son of

Elsie Tomkins with Ch. Duro Perfection as a puppy in 1912.

Mrs Foster's Ch. Ted. Her most famous early exhibit was Ch. Invincible who became a very strong influence within the kennels.

Probably the most famous dog of the 1930s was Ch. Harringay Remarkable. A son of Ch. Mendham Prince, Remarkable went on to beat all rival Yorkshire Terriers of his time. He was also the first Yorkshire Terrier to win Best Non-Sporting Dog in Show as well as winning the Toy Group at the Kennel Club Show.

Another famous breeder of this period was Lady Edith Windham-Dawson who had a number of champions to her credit from her Soham kennel; these included Ch. Victoria of Soham, Ch. Rose of the

Mrs A. Swan's Ch. Invincible in 1929. Winner of 14 CCs.

Lady Edith Windham-Dawson's Ch. Lord Randolph of Soham in 1930.

World, Ch. Thyra of Soham, Ch. James of Soham and Ch. Rose Crystal. Lady Windham-Dawson passed on much of her knowledge to her friend Miss A.E. Palmer before leaving Britain to settle in Ireland at the end of the war.

The 1940s to the Present Day

During the Second World War the showing of dogs was all but suspended. However, once the hostilities were over, interest in dog showing gradually increased and the Yorkshire Terrier in particular benefited greatly during this period. At this time travel was still a lot more difficult than it is today and so the interaction between breeders tended to be on a regional, rather than a countrywide basis. We will look first at the notable kennels in the north of England and Scotland and then look at the southern kennels' contributions during this post-war period.

Many of today's top specimens can trace their ancestry back

Mrs E. Stirk with Ch. Stirkean's Chota Sahib, winning the toy group at Blackpool Championship Show.

through many of the major kennels that have contributed to the breed over the years. This is particularly true of two very notable kennels which were developed by two ladies, Mrs Annie Swan and Mrs M. Crookshank. Mrs Swans' Invincia kennel was particularly noted for the richness of colour in the Yorkshire Terrier's coat while Mrs Crookshank's Johnstounburn kennel produced dogs renowned for their refined bone structure and pretty faces. Both of these kennels produced champion after champion and many of today's winning exhibits can be traced back to these two famous kennels.

It was in the 1920s that Mrs Swan first began breeding and showing Yorkshire Terriers, and so started a very successful career in the dog world working from her Stockport kennel. Mrs Swan bred many champions including Ch. Invincible who won a total of fourteen CCs. Because of her success and the growing fame of her kennels, Mrs Swan was persuaded by Jean Hopwood, a prominent figure in canine circles, of the benefit of having a prefix for her kennel's dogs. It seemed natural to use her most famous champion's name, and so the Invincia kennel began its contribution to the breed. Further prestige

Mrs A. Swan's Ch. Splendour of Invincia, winner of 17 CCs.

Mrs A. Swan's Ch. Delight of Invincia in 1939.

was brought to the kennel by the success of Ch. Eminent and Ch. Gudasgold. The main success came from the direct line of Ch. Invincible, who sired Ch. Delight of Invincia, who in turn went on to sire Invincia Masher who sired Ch. Splendour of Invincia who became a champion in 1947 and winner of a total of seventeen CCs. Mrs Swan also bred and campaigned Ch. Sunstar of Invincia and Ch. Adora of Invincia, both these champions being made up in 1952. To make it a hat trick for this year, a third Invincia bitch was made up when Ch. Tatiania of Invincia was successfully campaigned by Mrs Stirk of the Stirkeans kennel. Mrs Swan's kennel also produced another champion for Mrs Stirk, namely Ch. Stirkean Chota Sahib. Other exhibitors who benefited from Mrs Swan's breeding include Miss Martin, who owned and campaigned Ch. Hopwood Camelia and Mrs D. Beech of the Deebees kennel who owned and campaigned Ch. Martini in 1957, the first of many champions for Mrs Beech. Much of Mrs Swan's success was due to her dedication and great love for the breed, in particular her kennel was praised for dogs with coats noted for their rich, golden-tan and steel-blue colours.

29

Mrs A. Swan with Ch. Adora of Invincia and Ch. Sunstar of Invincia. Judge: Mr A. Coats of Martynwyns Yorkies.

At the same time that the Invincia kennel was having such success, Mrs Crookshank began breeding further north with stock that was completely unrelated to Mrs Swan's kennel. Mrs Crookshank started her interest breeding from her residence, Johnstounburn House, on the outskirts of Edinburgh, and named her kennels after the house. Looking for a pet companion Mrs Crookshank purchased a bitch whom she registered at the Kennel Club as Hazy of Johnstounburn. It was Hazy who became the foundation brood-bitch for the Edinburgh kennel that was to have such a major influence on the breed. Mrs Crookshank had a number of successes, both as a breeder and exhibitor, producing many champions from the mid-1940s right up to the mid-1960s. Probably the most famous of the kennel's dogs were Ch. and Ir. Ch. Mr Pim of Johnstounburn who achieved his championship status in 1950. Mr Pim, who was quite a small dog, weighing in at just 3 pounds (1.4kg), went on to achieve even greater success as a stud-dog and sired seven dogs who became champions during the 1950s. Three of these champions were campaigned by Mrs Crookshank herself, notably Ch. Myrtle of Johnstounburn, Ch. Primbron of Johnstounburn and Ch. Pipet of Johnstounburn. Besides his influence

*Mrs M. Crookshank's Int. Ch. Mr Pim of Johnstounburn. Sire to 7
British champions.*

within the Johnstounburn kennel through his use as a stud-dog
he made his mark within many other kennels, particularly in Scotland. The other champions that he sired were his first champion
progeny Ch. Wee Eve of Yadnum, Ch. Burantheas Angel Bright, Ch.

*Mrs M. Crookshank with her famous Ch. Pimbron of
Johnstounburn.*

Burantheas Doutelle and Ch. Prim of Johnstounburn who with Ch.
Primbron of Johnstounburn, shared the same dam, Lady of the Lake,
though they were produced in different litters.

Besides the success of Mr Pim, the Johnstounburn kennel had
many other successes in the show ring and bred Ch. Tufty of Johnstounburn, Ch. Medium of Johnstounburn and Ch. Minerva of Johnstounburn. In addition to this success must be added the success of the
many breeders who have used Johnstounburn stock in their breeding
schemes to produce many show winners. The Johnstounburn kennel
produced many fine dogs with excellent bone structures and conformation which, when finally combined with the fruits of Mrs Swan's
breeding, produced even more fine champions.

The original fusion of these two established but unrelated kennels,
Invincia and Johnstounburn, occurred at the Pagnell kennel in
Hooton, Yorkshire. The Pagnell kennel's owners, Mr and Mrs Vic
Groom purchased Prism of Johnstounburn as a foundation brood
from Mrs Crookshank and this bitch was mated to Ch. Burgwallis'

Ch. Tinker of Glendonian, owned by Mrs Gutridge. Great-grandsire of Ch. and Ir. Ch. Mr Pim of Johnstounbourn.

Mary Lowrie with Ch. Pipit of Johnstounburn (1950s).

Little Nip who was owned by Mary Betton. Little Nip was the grandson of Ch. Splendour of Invincia who had sired Little Nips's father Burgwallis Waggie. The union of Prism of Johnstounburn with Champion Little Nip produced a couple of future champions. The daughter of this union, Ch. Pagnell Prima Donna of Wiske had a remarkable career with her new owner Mrs K. Renton, and has the distinction of being the first Yorkshire Terrier to win Best in Show at an All-Breed Championship Show. The son was sold to Mrs Betton and registered under her own prefix as Burgwallis Vikki. He became a champion in 1960, one year later than his famous litter-sister.

Four years after the original mating, a repeat mating of Prism of Johnstounburn to Ch. Little Nip produced another famous dog for the Pagnell kennels. This was Ch. Pagnell Peter Pan who won a Reserve CC at Cruft's in 1963 when he was just thirteen months old. He returned the following year to win the Cruft's Best of Breed over the bitch winner Ch. Minerva of Johnstounburn. Ch. Pagnell Peter

Hilda and Les Griffiths' very famous champion, Ch. Beechrise Superb, sire to 7 British champions.

34

Hilda and Les Griffiths' Ch. Beechrise Superb at the age of 9 months.

Pan went on to mirror his elder sister's achievement by winning the Best in Show title at an All-Breeds Championship Show. From the show ring he then transferred his success to the siring of some excellent offspring. Unfortunately he was not at stud for long before he was exported to Japan, but although he did not leave many puppies behind he certainly produced some excellent ones with many of his own winning qualities. One of his sons, Ch. Pagnell Blue Peter, was campaigned and made up by the Grooms in 1967; another son, Lambsgrove Pinnochio was a CC winner in Britain for his owner and breeder Eva Lamb before leaving for the United States and becoming an American Champion. Prior to his departure Pinnochio sired a champion son, Ch. Tolcarne Brandy Soda who in turn went on to sire another champion, Ch. Tolcarne Drambuie. Both dogs were owned and bred by Olive Wood.

Ch. Pagnell Peter Pan's two most famous sons were probably Ch. Beechrise Superb owned and campaigned in 1966 by Les and Hilda Griffiths and Ch. Heavenly Blue of Wiske owned and made up in

Ch. Murose Exquisite, bred and owned by Mrs E. Burton.

1967 by Mr and Mrs Palframan. Both these dogs inherited their father's remarkable dominance and passed this quality on through their own offspring to future generations. This was certainly evident at the Griffiths's Beechrise kennel at Hemsworth, Pontifract, where they had bred Ch. Beechrise Superb from their own bitch Beechrise Pixie with Ch. Pagnell Peter Pan as sire. Ch. Beechrise Superb went on to sire seven British champions between the late 1960s and mid-1970s leaving his own stamp on the breed. These were Ch. Dandini Jim, Ch. Murose Storm, Ch. Gerjoy Royal Flea, Ch. Skyrona Blue Victoria, Ch. Toytop Tango, Ch. Blairsville Aristocrat, and Ch. Beechrise Surprise. The Griffiths also owned and campaigned Ch. Swank of Beechrise, Ch. Shaun of Beechrise and Ch. Souvenir of Beechrise; their other champion made up in 1979 was Ch. Beechrise Sweet Solitaire who was home-bred.

In 1968, Ch. Murose Storm, a son of Ch. Beechrise Superb, was the first champion of the well-established Murose kennel of Mrs Burton who went on to produce a number of home-bred champions from her

Chesterfield kennel. Ch. Murose Storm sired Ch. Murose Wee Pippa who went on to produce three champions: Ch. Murose Exquisite, Ch. Brascaysh Bezzer of Murose and Ch. Empress of Murose. Also to the credit of Mrs Burton's breeding are Ch. Murose Illustrious and his son Ch. Murose Masterpiece.

The late Joyce Blamire, along with her husband Ave of the well-known Wykebank kennel, produced Ch. Dandini Jim, another of the sons of Beechrise Superb, who was made up in 1968. Other successes then followed with Ch. Wykebank Super Solitaire, Ch. Wykebank Amethyst, Ch. Wykebank Impeccable, Ch. Wykebank Startime, Ch. Wykebank Tinkerbell – who was a winner of the Best in Show title at an All-Breed Championship Show – and finally, Ch. Wykebank Wild Rose who was owned by Mrs K. Henderson. After the death of Joyce, Ave remarried to Janice Bunting who made up Ch. Maritoys Midnight Rose in 1985.

Ch. Heavenly Blue of Wiske was another well-known son of Ch. Pagnell Peter Pan and he was bred by Kitty Renton, a breed enthusiast based at Harrogate in Yorkshire. Besides breeding Ch. Heavenly

Joyce Blamires with her Ch. Wykebank Startime.

Blue of Wiske Mrs Renton owned many beautiful champions during the 1950s and 1960s. These included Ch. Pagnell Prima Donna of Wiske, Ch. Doone of Wiske (who was the mother of Ch. Heavenly Blue of Wiske), Ch. Sundance of Wiske, Ch. Romance of Wiske, Ch. Templevale Niaissmo of Wiske and Ch. Templevale Jessica of Wiske. Ch. Heavenly Blue of Wiske was owned by Mr and Mrs Palframan of the Plantation Hall kennel in Bradford and they campaigned him to his title. As a stud-dog he sired Ch. Brave Warrior of Naylenor who was owned by Phillip and Kim Naylor of the Naylenor kennels. The

Mr P. Naylor with his Ch. Naylenor Magic Moment.

Mr B. Lister with his first champion, Ch. Blairsville Tinkerbell; the judge Mrs K. Renton of the Wiske fame and Mr D. Stroud with his first champion, Ch. Macstroud's Sir Gay.

Naylors campaigned him successfully in 1971. After this, Ch. Brave Warrior of Naylenor was himself put to stud and sired a home-bred winner, Ch. Naylenor Blue Monarch. Other wins for the Naylors included Ch. Naylenor Magic Moment and Ch. Naylenor Crown in the Jewel.

Another successful kennel is the Blairsville owned by Brian and Rita Lister and based at Pudsey near Leeds in Yorkshire. Their first champion was Ch. Blairsville Tinkerbell in 1967 and she was the daughter of the foundation bitch they purchased from the Leodian kennel of Mary Henry. The Leodian lines had been founded almost entirely on Invincia stock direct from Mrs Swan. The Listers' second success was Ch. Blairsville Boy Wonder, who was Tinkerbell's full brother, and was closely followed by two of his daughters, Ch. Blairsville Shirene, in 1970 and Ch. Blairsville Samantha, in 1971. When Ch. Blairsville Tinkerbell retired for maternal duties she produced a son by Ch. Beechrise Superb who became Ch. Blairsville Aristocrat in 1970. Ch. Blairsville Shirene was mated with only one outcross, namely Richard Wardell's Ch.

Whisperdales Tamujin, and the result was Ch. Blairsville Most Royale, the dam of their famous Ch. Blairsville Royal Seal. Both mother and son earned the highly creditable distinction of being Best in Show winners at an All-Breed Championship Show and the son, Ch. Blairsville Royal Seal, went on to collect fifty CCs after being championed in 1975 and was the first Yorkshire Terrier to make a half-century of wins.

After retiring Royal Seal, the Listers made up Ch. Blairsville Gaiety in 1980 and went on to breed their last champion, Ch. Blairsville Royal Pardon, who was campaigned by Lyn and Kevin Gillespie in 1984. The Gillespies also bred three champions during the mid-1980s: Ch. Evening Blue, Ch. Christmas Fable and Ch. Royalties Reflex owned by Mrs Y. Windsor.

There are a number of other kennels and exhibitors who are well worth a mention for their contribution to the Yorkshire Terrier breed in the north of England during the post-war years. Much early success in the show ring was achieved by Dr Mair and his wife during the 1940s and 1950s. Travelling from their Sunderland home, Dr and Mrs Mair owned and campaigned four champions: Ch. Vemair Parkview Preview, Ch. Vemair Principal Boy, Ch. Vemair Spider and, in 1955, Ch. Vemair Uncle Sam.

Another keen exhibitor and breeder was Mrs G. Sykes, who owned the Skyrona Kennels based in Sheffield, Yorkshire. Good home-breeding produced the kennel's first champion when Ch. Skyrona Blue Prince was campaigned in 1964. He went on to achieve more success by siring Ch. Skyrona Blue Bobby of Stremglen and Ch. Skryona Blue Girl. After achieving her champion status, Blue Girl was mated to Ch. Beechrise Superb and another champion was the result – Ch. Skyrona Blue Victoria – who was made up by Mrs Sykes in 1970.

Sheffield is also the home of another successful kennel, the Carmady kennel, owned by Mrs Joan Parkin. The Carmady's show success began in 1975 with the making up of their Ch. Carmady Little Henry. He was followed by Ch. Carmady Marcus and Ch. Carmady Cassius who fathered the kennels' fourth champion, Ch. Carmady Annie, who was made up in 1988.

Another Yorkshire kennel to achieve high standards during the 1980s was the Coletts kennel in Hull. This kennel is run by husband and wife team Terry and Mary Cole. The first champion to come from the Coles' breeding programme was Ch. Souvenir of Beechrise who was successfully campaigned by his owners, Mr and Mrs Griffiths, in

Mrs Hepworth with her Ch. Millfield Mandy (left), the judge
Mrs M. Burfield and Mrs G. Sykes with her Ch. Skyrona Blue
Prince.

1980. Further success came through the Coles campaigning their home-bred Ch. Coletts Charmaine and her son, Ch. Coletts Gold Sovereign. In addition to this, several foreign champions have come from the Coletts kennel.

Richard Haynes who has been my friend for many years and whose knowledge of breeders past and present has been a great help to me, bred Ch. Ebracum Paladin closely following the Johnstounburn line. In Scotland, when writing of the many lovely dogs from the Johnstounburn line, it is important to mention Ch. My Precious Joss, who was made up in 1965. He was bred by Mrs C. Flockhart of the Silverknowes affix from a bitch sired by Lillyhill Gem of Hintwood, a well-known little stud owned by Mary Lowrie whose excellent kennel did so much to popularize the breed in Scotland. The dam to Ch. My Precious Joss, Bonny Jean – a granddaughter of Ch. and Ir. Ch. Mr Pim of Johnstounburn – was mated to Ch. Pimbron of Johnstounburn, and Ch. My Precious Joss was the result.

Ch. My Precious Joss's line was further accentuated when Mrs Joyce W. Mann started her kennel under the Craigsbank affix. As a result of line-breeding from Johnstounburn through Ch. My

41

Precious Joss the strain was finally mixed with the Pagnell line within the Craigsbank kennel. The result was the kennels' first champion, Ch. Craigsbank Blue Cinder, who was made up in 1977. Further successes for Mrs Mann's breeding followed in the 1980s with Ch.

Mrs Mary Cole with her Ch. Colletts Charmain.

Mr J.R. Hayne's Ch. Eburacum Paladin.

Joyce Mann's Ch. Craigsbank Blue Cinders.

43

Mrs Overtt's Ch. Wee Blue Atom in 1950.

Craigsbank Miss Dior, Ch. Craigsbank Stormy Affair and Ch. Craigsbank She's a Lady. The last two of these were owned and campaigned by Jackie Leslie who showed her third champion in 1987. This was Ch. Annalon Love Letter, bred by Mrs. A. Swaine-Wise.

Another notable Scottish kennel was that of the late Mr D. Peck of the Glengonner affix, who made up Ch. Glamour Boy of Glengonner in 1961. Mr Peck then used Glamour Boy to sire a second champion for him, Ch. Ruswell Chorus Girl of Brendali, who was owned and campaigned by Mrs R. Marshall in 1965.

In the south of England the breed was dominated by a completely unrelated influence emanating from the famous Ravelin kennel at Romford in Essex, which was established by Nell and Jack Latliff in the early 1950s. This kennel produced several champions which were, in the main, campaigned by other kennels. The first of these was Mrs W. Overt's Ch. Wee Blue Atom who was made up in 1951. Although not a champion himself, his father, Little Boy Blue, owned by Mr Coats, went on to sire two more champions for the Ravelin kennel, namely, Ch. Martynwyns Debonaire for Mr Coat and Champion June's Boy for the Latliffs themselves. Another successful studdog for the Ravelin kennel was Ravelin Little Jimmy who sired two British champions and whose name can be traced in the ancestry of many of today's winners. Two successful bitches bred by the Latliffs were Ch. Martynwyns Adora who was campaigned by Mrs Seymour in 1955 and Ch. Ravelin Gaiety Boy who was campaigned by Miss P. Noakes in 1958.

Ch. Ravelin Gaiety Boy was a very welcome addition to Miss

44

Mrs N. Latliff's Ch. June's Boy.

Noakes's Phirno kennel, which was based at Southend in Essex. He went on to sire two future champions for his kennel: Ch. Phirno Magic Moment, who was successfully campaigned by Miss Noakes in 1964, and her half-sister Ch. Whisperdales Phirno Carmen, who was owned by Richard Wardell and made up in 1965. Other successes for the Phirno kennel included Ch. Blue Bell, Ch. Phirno St George and Ch. Phirno Lord Gay. Mr Wardell was also successful at his Whisperdales kennel when his home-bred Ch. Whisperdales Tamujin was made up in 1964 followed by his daughter Ch. Whisperdales Deebees Half Penny in 1972. Working in close contact with the Ravelin kennel was the Martynwyns kennel owned by Mr Coats and very successful during the late 1940s and through the 1950s. Mr Coats bred and owned Ch. Blue Dolly and campaigned Ch. Martynwyns Surprise of Atherleigh, bred by Mr Hayes and Ch. Martynwyns Debonaire, bred by Mr and Mrs Latliff at the Ravelin kennel. Other breeding successes came with Ch. Martynwyns Little Marvel, Ch. Martynwyns Wee Teddy and Ch. Martynwyns Golden Girl who was

Mr R. Wardell with his Ch. Whisperdale's Phirno Carmen. Judge: Emma Wilkinson.

campaigned by her owner Mrs J. Montgomery at the Jacaranda Kennels. This was Mrs Montgomery's first champion and was quickly followed a year later in 1952 by her home-bred dog Ch. Jacaranda Beauty. Another home-bred success was Ch. Jacaranda Blue Mischief who was made up in 1962; Mrs Montgomery also owned and campaigned Ch. Ozmilion Destiny to her title in 1976.

Mrs C. Hutchin of the Progresso fame had much success both as a breeder and an exhibitor. Her first success came with Ch. Coolgorm Chloe whom she took to her title in 1958. This achievement was followed just one year later by her first home-bred success, Ch. Don Carlos of Progresso, who was a son of Ch. Martynwyns Wee Teddy. A son of Ch. Don Carlos of Progresso was Ch. Progress of Progresso, who went on to sire Ch. Progresso Lover Boy, both father and son being home-bred and campaigned by Mrs Hutchin during the early 1960s. Mrs Hutchin also owned and campaigned three other champions, each of whom had a Progresso stud-dog as his sire. These were Ch. Melody Maker of Embyll, bred by Mr W.E. Everett, Ch. Progresso Pearl bred by Mr Brown and Ch. Progresso Prospect bred by Mr Langley. Besides her success in Britain, Mrs Hutchin exported many excellent Yorkshire Terriers who became champions and often contributed to the breeding programmes in their new countries.

Connie Hutchin's first home-bred champion, Ch. Don Carlos of Progresso.

In 1952 Mrs Ethel Munday of the Yadnum kennel, and one-time secretary of the Yorkshire Terrier Club, made up her first of many champions. This was Ch. Wee Eve of Yadnum who was a daughter of the famous Ch. and Ir. Ch. Mr Pim of Johnstounburn and was bred by Mr A. Scott. Further success followed for Mrs Munday during the 1950s and 1960s with Ch. Eoforwic Envoy of Yadnum bred by Mrs Prosser, Ch. Midnight Gold of Yadnum bred by Mrs Donaldson, Ch. Moonglow of Yadnum bred by Mrs Sharp, Ch. Elmsglade Galahad of Yadnum bred by Mrs Slade, and Ch. Golden Button of Yadnum and Ch. Luna Star of Yadnum, both being home-bred.

Miss Vera Munday, a daughter of Mrs Munday and joint owner of the Yadnum affix made her first champion, Ch. Pretty Debbie of

Yadnum in 1969, who was bred by Mrs G. Bulgin. Ch. Super Fine of Yadnum followed in 1971 and he was home-bred. Other successes followed for Miss Munday during the rest of the 1970s and into the 1980s. These included Ch. Mycariad Ragged Robin of Yadnum bred by Miss V. Child; Ch. Robina Gay of Yadnum who was home-bred; Ch. Azurene Moss Rose of Yadnum and Ch. Azurene Corduroy of Yadnum, both bred by Mrs G. Bulgin, and home-bred Ch. Yadnum Regal Fair.

During the 1950s Mrs M. Burfield started her Buranthea kennels at Northolt in Middlesex and achieved much success with her breeding by using stock with a background of Invincia, Johnstounburn and Soham lines and breeding many successful show specimens. Her first two home-bred champions both shared Ch. and Ir. Ch. Mr Pim of Johnstounburn as their sire, they were Ch. Burantheas Angel Bright and Ch. Burantheas Doutelle who were both exported to America. Mrs Burfield introduced the Clu-Mor line through Ir. Ch. Picolo Patrico who was the sire of the well-known Ch. Burantheas Saint Malachy, who was made up in 1964. Further success in the show ring came when Ch. Burantheas Luscious Lady was made up in 1967; this was to be her last champion.

Mrs Rossitar, now known as Mrs D. Hillman, bred from Johnstounburn and Buranthea lines and her first home-bred champion was Ch. Yorkford Rupert Bear in 1963, who was followed a year later by Ch. Yorkfold McPickle. Ch. Prim of Johnstounburn who, in 1950, was the very first champion Mrs Hillman made up, was bred by Mr Brown and had been purchased from Mrs Crookshank.

Mrs E. Stirk of the Stirkeans kennel started in the early 1950s with the Invincia line and made her first champion, Ch. Titanina of Invincia, in 1952, followed by Ch. Stirkeans Chota Sahib a year later, both bred by Mrs Swan. Ch. Stirkeans Kandy Boy was the first home-bred champion for the Stirkeans kennel based at Worthing in Sussex and was campaigned in 1955. Many other champions followed during the rest of the 1950s and 1960s; these were Ch. Stirkeans Faustina owned by Mrs D. Beech, Ch. Stirkeans Rhapsody, Ch. Stirkeans Astonoff Horatio bred by Mrs. M. Hetherington, Ch. Stirkeans Puff Puffin, Ch. Stirkeans Mr Timms, Ch. Stirkeans Rennie and Ch. Stirkeans Gerrards Little Guy who was bred by Miss E. Thomas.

Mrs D. Beech started her Deebees kennel directly on Invincia lines and her first champion, Martini, was made up in 1957 and bred by Mrs Swan; her second was Ch. Deebees Stirkeans Faustina, bred by Mrs Stirk. These early champions were just the beginnings of a long run of champions that continues even to this day.

Mr B. Lister with his famous Ch. Blairsville Royal Seal; judge Mrs D. Hillman; and Mrs D. Beech with Ch. Wellshim Madam of Deebees.

During the 1960s the Deebees kennel campaigned many home-bred champions: Ch. Deebees Campari, Ch. Deebees Isa La Bela, Ch. Deebees Hot Toddy, Ch. Deebees Caromia, Ch. Deebees Little Dodo, Ch. Deebees Doncella and Ch. Deebees Gold Penny. Mrs Beech's first champion of the 1970s came when Ch. Deebees Beebee was made up in 1971. Ch. Deebees Beebee was bred by Mrs Pitcher and was a winner of Best in Show at an All-Breed Championship Show before being exported to America. The next success came a year later when Ch. Whisperdales Deebees Halfpenny was campaigned by her owner Mr W. Wardell. Then came a run of home-bred and campaigned successes for the kennel: Ch. Deebees Cornish Echo, his daughter Ch. Deebees Penny Rose and Ch. Deebees Speculation. Mrs A. Shinwell became a joint owner of the Deebees affix and helped to breed and campaign further champions for the kennels: Ch. Wellshim Madam of Deebees, followed by her son Ch. Deebees My Fascination, Ch. Deebees Golden Delight, Ch. Deebees Dominic and Ch. Deebees Golden Fancy who having been made up in 1988 was the Deebees kennel's nineteenth British champion.

Working in Birmingham Mr and Mrs H. Oakley began their

Mrs S. Chiswell and Mrs E. Leyton's Ch. Chandas Inspiration.

Candytops kennel in the late 1960s with mainly Deebees stock and have continually been successful ever since. The Oakleys purchased their first show male, Candytops Deebees Peter Piper from an all-Deebees line and produced their first champion, Ch. Candytops Blue Peter who was campaigned in 1972. Their next successes were in 1976 with Ch. Katie Fare of Candytops, who was bred by Mr F. Morris, and home-bred Ch. Candytops Chantilly Lace. These were quickly followed by Ch. Candytops Strawberry Fair, Ch. Candytops Raffles and Ch. Candytops Candy Man. In 1977, the Oakleys introduced the Blairsville strain by mating their own Ch. Candytops Chantilly Lace to Ch. Blairsville Royal Seal and produced Ch. Candytops Cavalcadia, who was made a champion in 1981 along with his own daughter Ch. Candytops Fair Delight. A second offspring of Cavalcadia was his son Ch. Royal Cascade, who in turn went on to sire Ch. Candytops Amelia Fair, who was followed by Ch. Candytops Royal Sovereign.

Another Birmingham kennel to achieve success was owned jointly by Mr and Mrs Chiswell along with Mrs Edna Leyton. They owned, and in 1977 campaigned, Ch. Chevawn Sweet Shona who was bred by Mrs Campion. Ch. Chandas Shona's Girl and Ch. Chandas Inspiration were both home-bred and became champions during the 1980s.

My own kennel, Ozmilion, based in South London, has over the years given me a great deal of satisfaction and pleasure. At the age of eleven I came to live with my aunt. She had three beautiful Yorkshire Terriers, a breed that I had always loved and admired. They were related to the Martynwyns and the Progresso line; one bitch came from Ir. Ch. Count Heystbury of the Johnstournburn line and they were bought from George Tomkins and his daughter, Elsie Tomkins. I was shown a picture of the Johnstounburn champions sitting together; that same picture now hangs on my wall and is a constant reminder of how I came to start my own line. The name Ozmilion was made up because my family called me Oz and I wanted a million Yorkshire Terriers. So the name Ozmilion (with one 'l') came about. I had a great deal of help and support from my dear friends such as the late Mary Lowrie of the famous Lillyhill Yorkies, Margaret Howes and Elsie Tomkins and her father. The two most dear friends Hilda Griffiths and Richard Haynes were the people who persuaded me to show my Ozmilion Yorkshire Terriers. With the help and guidance from Mrs Lowrie I became the proud owner of the daughters of Ch. Pimbron of Johnstounburn and Ch. My Precious Joss and in turn they were mated to grandsons of Prism of Johnstounburn and great-grandsons of Ch. Splendour of Invincia. It was then that the dream which I had had for so many years started to take shape and grow. My first champion, Ch. My Imagination, was born on the 14 July 1970 and his first show was the Manchester Championship Show on 14 March 1971, where he won his class. So began my association with the show ring.

Since then there have been thirty-four champions with the

Mrs M. Crookshank's Johnstounburn champions.

Mary Lowrie with the author and his Int. Ch. Ozmilion Modesty in 1974.

Ozmilion affix in England, including my own twenty-five champions. In the male line there have been Ch. Ozmilion My Imagination, Ch. and Ir. Ch. Ozmilion Jubilation. Ch. Ozmilion Distinction, Ch. Ozmilion Premonition and his two sons, Ch. Ozmilion Devotion and Ch. Ozmilion Tradition, and his son Ch. Ozmilion Ovation; Ch. Ozmilion Expectation, Ch. Ozmilion Invitation, Ch. Ozmilion Admiration and his son Ch. Ozmilion Dedication – the top dog of 1987 and currently the top-winning Yorkshire Terrier of all time and a winner of 52 CCs. HIs son is Ch. and Ir. Ch. Ozmilion Sensation and his son, Ch. Ozmilion My Infatuation. In the bitches there have been Ch. and Ir. Ch. Ozmilion Modesty, Ch. Ozmilion Justimagine, Ch. Ozmilion Dream Maker owned and campaigned by my sister-in-law Veronica Sameja-Hilliard; Ch. Ozmilion Destiny, owned and campaigned by Mrs Montgomery; Ch. Ozmilion Exageration the only daughter of Ch. Ozmilion Modesty; Ch. Ozmilion Heart's Desire, Ch. Ozmilion Flames of Desire, Ch. Ozmilion Flames of Passion, Ch. Ozmilion Love Romance, Ch. Ozmilion Dance of Romance, Ch. Ozmilion Hopelessly

The author's 20 Ozmilion champions.

in Love, Ch. Ozmilion Kisses of Fire, Ch. Ozmilion Irresistable Love, and Ch. Ozmilion Aspects of Love. I feel very proud to know that my champions have in turn bred further champions for myself and for other kennels. Ch. and Ir. Ch. Ozmilion Jubilation has sired fourteen British champions and Ch. Ozmilion Heart's Desire is dam to five British champions.

Mrs Sameja-Hilliard owned and campaigned Ch. Ozmilion Dream Maker, her first champion, in 1977, and she then followed this with home-bred champions. Ch. Verolian Just A Jewel with Ozmilion was followed by the record-holder in bitches, Ch. Verolian Temptress with Ozmilion, with thirty-nine CCs to her credit. As yet there is not another bitch that has come even remotely close to beating this record

Veronica Sameja-Hilliard's Ch. Verolian Temptress with Ozmilion.

and credit must be given to her for her showmanship and determination. Then followed Ch. Verolian Appreciation at Ozmilion, Ch. Verolian The Adverturess at Ozmilion and latest champion to date, Ch. Verolian Al Pacino who was campaigned in 1989.

Mr Joe Magri owned, and in 1983 campaigned, Ch. Bee Bee MiBlase, which he followed a year later with Ch. Emotions of Ozmilion at Rozamie. He also bred Rozamie Endless Love who was campaigned by Mr B. Downey and Mr R. Enz in 1989.

Another kennel to take advantage of the Johnstounburn and Invincia lines was the West Country establishment owned by Mr and Mrs Jack Knight of the Whitecross affix. They extensively mated their original bitches, who had some Invincia breeding, either to Ch. Pimbron of Johnstounburn or to Ch. Splendour of Invincia. The combination of Pimbron bitches to Splendour or his sons proved outstandingly successful, bringing together the best of the two lines.

The Whitecross line was just starting to reap the benefits of years of careful breeding when fate dealt an untimely blow with the death of Mr Knight. As it was he who had been the real driving force behind them, the kennel was dispersed.

Mr David Stroud was founding his Macstrouds kennel at this time and a number of Whitecross dogs and bitches formed the new breeding nucleus that was to prove a great success during the 1960s and 1970s. Nearly all the Macstrouds have a very large amount of Whitecross blood in their veins. These include such well-known names as Ch. and Ir. Ch. Macstroud's Sir Gay, Ch. and Ir. Ch. Macstroud's Noble Lad, Ch. Macstroud's High Society, Ch. Macstroud Noble Boy and Ch. Macstroud Blue Soldier. There was another very famous Macstroud Whitecross Dandini, who, although he did not gain his title, sired a considerable number of champions during the late 1960s and early 1970s, including Ch. Dorrits Macstroud Hot Toddy for Mrs D. Baynes. Three famous daughters of Dandini were owned by Mary Hayes: Ch. Chantmarles Mycariad Wild Silk, Ch. Chantmarles Snuff Box and Ch. Chantmarles Miss Boniface, the latter two being bred by Mrs Hayes. In addition, Ch. Chantmarles Snuff Box was campaigned in 1969 and became a winner of the Best in Show at an All-Breeds Championship Show. Ch. Chantmarles Mycariad Wild Silk was bred by Vera Childe for Mrs Hayes and Miss Childe also bred Ch. Mycariad Ragged Robin of Yadnum who was made up by Miss Munday in 1972.

One of the most successful kennels in South Wales belongs to Mary and John Hayes of the Chantmarles Yorkshire Terriers; they have an impressive string of champions bearing the Chantmarles affix. Besides their three early champions, sired by Macstroud Whitecross Dandini, the Chantmarles have bred a large number of champions, many of whom they have campaigned themselves during the 1970s and 1980s. Their list of champions to date includes Ch. Chantmarles Sauce Box, Ch. Chantmarles Sash Box, Ch. Chantmarles Elegance, Ch. Chantmarles Stowaway, Ch. Chantmarles Dolly Dimple, Ch. Chantmarles Proper Madam, Ch. Chantmarles Celebrity, Ch. Chantmarles Best Intentions and also Ch. Chantmarles Debutant for Mr P. Boot, Ch. Chantmarles Rose Bowl and Ch. Chantmarles Wild Rose for Mrs D. Lorenz, Ch. Chantmarles Candy for Mr and Mrs Haythornthwaite, Ch. Chantmarles President of Yat for Messrs Downey and Enz, Ch. Chantmarles Curiosity, Ch. Chantmarles Chivalry and finally Ch. Chantmarles Gaiety, who in 1989 became the nineteenth British champion for the Chantmarles kennels. The Hayes have also bred a number of overseas champions.

Mr B.Downey and Mr R. Enz's Ch. Chantmarles President of Yat.

Mrs B. Charlton-Haw with her two champions, Ch. Sir Lancelot of Astolat and his sister Ch. Elaine of Astolat, in 1958.

Mrs D. Baynes with her Ch. My Sweet Susanne (left);
Mrs J. Montgomery the judge; and Mrs D. Mayall with her Ch.
Leyham Mascot, made up in 1961.

Besides the major kennels with their great strings of successes there have been many southern breeders who have contributed to the breed by their efforts. Some of these are mentioned in the remaining paragraphs. During the 1950s Margret Howes of the Sehow affix and present joint owner, along with Mrs D. Millman, of the Johnstoun-burn affix, campaigned and owned Ch. Sehow Independent who had been bred by Miss P. Marther. The late 1950s also saw a double success for Mrs P. Charlton-Haw who bred and campaigned Ch. Sir Lancelot of Astolat and his litter-sister Ch. Elaine of Astolat.

Mrs Seymour had success in campaigning Ch. Martynwyn Adora to her title in 1955; further success came with her home-bred champions, Ch. Blue Orchid of Hilfore in 1957 and Ch. Adora Junior of Hilfore, who was a daughter of Martynwyns Adora, in 1961.

Another winner in 1961 was Ch. Leyham Mascot who was bred and owned by Mrs D. Mayall who also bred Ch. Dorrits Leyham Scampie for Mrs D. Baynes who campaigned three other champions. These were home-bred bitches Ch. My Sweet Susanne in 1960 and her daughter Ch. Dorrits Susanne's Treasure in 1967, followed in 1971 by Ch. Dorrits Macstroud Hot Toddy who was bred by Mr D.

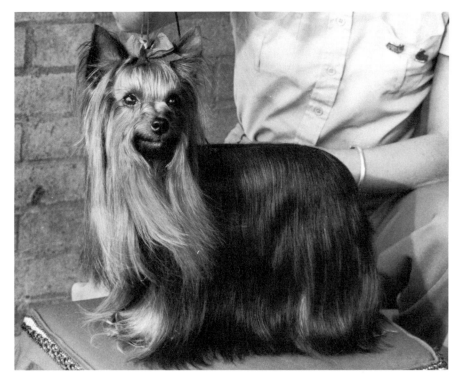

Mrs J. Reader's Ch. Jackread Appleblossom.

Stroud. Using a bitch from the Whitecross breeding proved successful for Mrs Ivy Millard as she bred and campaigned Ch. Nelmila
Berryfield Beauty in 1969.

The early 1970s saw a double success for Mrs D. Johnson and her
Lyndoney kennel with home-bred dogs Ch. Lyndoney Timothy Tup-
pence and Ch. Lyndoney Krishna.

In 1974, Mrs E. Bardwell and Mr and Mrs S. Bardwell owned and
campaigned Ch. Jackread Whiskey A Go Go of Stewell, bred by Mrs
J. Reader who also bred and owned Ch. Jackread Apple Blossom. Ch.
Jackread Whiskey A Go Go of Stewell sired Ch. Stewell Moonstorm
who went on to sire home-bred Ch. Stewell Storm Queen who was
made up in 1989. The Bardwells' other home-bred champion was Ch.
Stewell Soul Singer who was made up in 1984.

Mrs Gladys Da Silva began breeding during the 1960s and had a
double success in 1978 with two champions being made up: Ch.
Typros The Devil of Spicebox and Ch. Typros Evening Star. Further

Mrs E. Bardwell and Mr and Mrs S. Bardwell's Ch. Stewell Soul Singer.

Mr and Mrs J. Wells' Ch. Keriwell Flirtation.

success came during the 1980s with Ch. Typros Royal Splendour and Ch. Typros Lady of Elegance, and a good start to the 1990s came with Ch. Typros New Generation being made up in 1990.

During the late 1980s Mr and Mrs J. Wells bred and owned Ch. Keriwell Flirtation and Ch. and Ir. Ch. Keriwell Reflection. They also bred Ch. and Ir. Ch. Keriwell True Love, who was owned by Mr and Mrs J. Clelland.

Unfortunately, no text can do justice to and include all those who have contributed to the show history of Yorkshire Terriers over the years. I have tried to include those whose influence has been greatest but must apologise for those that have been omitted. Finally, there have been some excellent kennels and breeders who have produced many superb Yorkshire Terriers without becoming involved in the world of show dogs but have done much to ensure the excellent quality of the Yorkshire Terriers we have today.

2

The Breed Standard

The Kennel Club is responsible for drawing up a Breed Standard for every breed of dog. This Standard is used as a guide for breeders, exhibitors and judges to refer to when working towards the goal of the perfect Yorkshire Terrier. The original Breed Standard for the Yorkshire Terrier was first drawn up and accepted by the Kennel Club in 1898 and it was this Standard that breeders had worked with until 1987 when a revised Breed Standard was issued. This new Breed Standard is now the guide for our breeding programmes and for the pursuit of excellence in the show ring. This Standard is, as yet, an ideal and not an exact description of any particular specimen of Yorkshire Terrier. It is open to many different interpretations by breeders, judges and exhibitors.

The UK Breed Standard

(Reproduced by kind permission of the Kennel Club of Great Britain)

General Appearance

Long coated, coat hanging quite straight and evenly down each side, a parting extending from nose to end of tail. Very compact and neat, carriage very upright conveying an important air. General outline conveying impression of vigorous and well-proportioned body.

Characteristics

Alert, intelligent toy terrier.

Temperament

Spirited with even disposition.

Head and Skull

Rather small and flat, not too prominent or round in skull, nor too long in muzzle; black nose.

Eyes

Medium, dark, sparkling, with sharp intelligent expression and placed to look directly forward. Not prominent. Edge of eyelids dark.

Ears

Small, V-shaped, carried erect, not too far apart, covered with short hair, colour very deep, rich tan.

Mouth

Perfect, regular and complete scissor bite, i.e. the upper teeth closely overlapping lower teeth and set square to the jaws. Teeth well placed with even jaws.

Neck

Good reach.

Forequarters

Well laid shoulders, legs straight, well covered with hair of rich golden tan a few shades lighter at ends than at roots, not extending higher on forelegs than elbow.

Body

Compact, with moderate spring of rib; good loin. Level back.

Hindquarters

Legs quite straight when viewed from behind, moderate turn of stifle. Well covered with hair of rich golden tan a few shades lighter at ends than at roots, not extending higher on hind legs than stifle.

Mrs M.D.Y. Lowrie's Ch. Pimbron of Johnstounburn.

Feet

Round; nails black.

Tail

Customarily docked to medium length with plenty of hair, darker blue in colour than rest of body, especially at the end of tail. Carried a little higher than level of back.

Gait/Movement

Free with drive; straight action front and behind, retaining level topline.

Coat

Hair on body moderately long, perfectly straight (not wavy), glossy;

fine silky texture, not woolly. Fall on head long, rich golden tan, deeper in colour at sides of head, about ear roots and on muzzle where it should be very long. Tan on head not to extend on to neck, nor must any sooty or dark hair intermingle with any of tan.

Colour

Dark steel blue (not silver blue), extending from occiput to root of tail, never mingled with fawn, bronze or dark hairs. Hair on chest rich, bright tan. All tan hair darker at the roots than in middle, shading to still lighter at tips.

Size

Weight up to 3.1kg (7lb).

Faults

Any departure from the foregoing points should be considered a fault and the seriousness with which the fault should be regarded should be in exact proportion to its degree.

Note

Male animals should have two apparently normal testicles fully descended into the scrotum.

Interpretation of the Standard

Character and Temperament

The character and temperament of the Yorkshire Terrier is probably the main reason for his phenomenal success as a pet companion, his outward friendly manner and liveliness being a constant joy to his owners.

Part of the Yorkshire terrier's character is an extension of his early origins as a ratter, this terrier aspect being apparent in his eager, fearless and inquisitive manner. A puppy's personality and character begins to be formed from a very young age and so it is important that they receive much love and encouragement to develop their healthy

Mr and Mrs K. Parker's Ch. Marshonia Top Secret.

curiosity and friendly disposition in these early stages. Although the Yorkshire Terrier should be fearless, he must also be obedient and in no way outwardly aggressive towards people and other dogs. Ideally the show dog will display his bright and intelligent character whilst showing a fearless and spirited disposition; most of all the successful show dog will be happy with his role and this enjoyment will shine through in his performance.

Nose

The nose should have a very dark and even pigmentation. A light nose is undesirable for showing and is due to breakdown in the pigmentation. This would be heavily marked down at show.

Eyes

The preferred Yorkshire Terrier eye is one that is almond shaped rather than round, as shaped eyes look more natural in the Yorkshire Terrier's face. These eyes should not be too big so that they dominate the face, but of a medium size. They should be dark with a uniform dark rim. The eyes should reflect the dog's character, and sparkle to show intelligence and curiosity with all around him. These expressive eyes should be forward-looking and attentive to the judge, when in the show ring.

Ears

The correct shape for the ears is V-shaped and not round at the tips; they must be small and erect and not set too far apart. The ears should be like thin leather but still have sufficient strength to keep them erect. They should be covered in deep, rich tan hair which should be trimmed to show the ears' shape.

Mouth

The show dog's mouth must be in excellent condition, his teeth must show a scissor bite. Both upper and lower jaws should consist of a

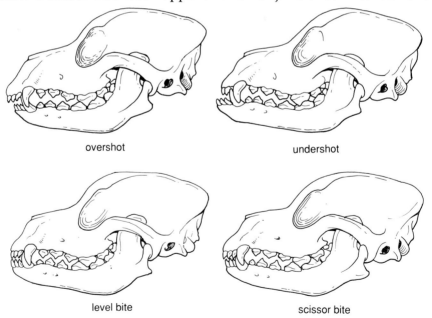

overshot

undershot

level bite

scissor bite

The Yorkshire Terrier's mouth and jaw, showing correct and incorrect formation.

complete set of teeth with the upper set closely overlapping the lower set of teeth. All the teeth should be sound, although any loss of teeth as a result of an accident would not be considered a fault. The teeth must be well placed and set square to the jaws and the jaws must be even. Neither an undershot mouth nor an overshot mouth has a place in the exhibition ring nor should they play a part in breeding programmes. Even if their offspring had regular mouths there would still be a high chance of the inferior mouth returning with future generations.

Neck

The neck should be well muscled but not coarse, with a good reach so that the head is carried proudly and not tacked on to his shoulders. The neck should also have a good range of movement, both from side to side and up and down. The neck must be well defined and great care should be taken by the owner to ensure the dog does not put on too much weight and so lose the neck's definition.

Forequarters

The dog's forequarters should show well-laid shoulders with straight forelegs which have the elbows close to the chest and which show a nice straight front when the dog is on the move. The forequarters should contribute to the dog's alert and proud stance, they must be straight and must not splay out or be turned in. The legs should be well covered with long rich golden hair a few shades lighter at the ends than at the roots. The tan should not extend any higher than the elbow on the forequarters.

Hindquarters

Whether the dog is standing still or on the move his hind legs should appear straight when viewed from the rear, that is, they should not turn inwards or turn outwards. When viewed from the side, the hind legs should show a slight turn to the stifle (knee). The feet should point forward, with the lower part of the leg leaning backwards then turning forwards from the knee. The hind legs should have a similar covering of hair to match the front pair, again the tan not extending higher than the stifle. If there are any dew-claws on the hind legs then it is better if they are removed as they serve no purpose and could

The author's Ch. Ozmilion Admiration.

catch on the dog's coat in the show ring. This also applies to the dew-claws on the forelegs and they should be removed very early in the animal's life.

Body

The Yorkshire Terrier's body should be well proportioned and compact with a good level back line which must remain level when the dog is on the move. The height at shoulder should be the same as at the rump. He will have a good short loin with well-developed muscles. The chest should have a good curvature of rib with a relatively wide front.

Feet

The feet should be small and neat with little spread and of a roundish shape. The nails will be black in colour and should be well trimmed so as not to impair the dog's movement; the hair on the feet should also be kept trimmed.

Tail

The Yorkshire's tail is by custom docked to medium length and will be carried slightly higher than the line of the back. The tail should have plenty of hair which should be a darker shade of blue than the rest of the body, especially at the tip. Although an undocked tail is permissible in the show ring it is not usually well received by the judges as it detracts from the overall pleasing impression of the dog.

Gait

The dog's movement should be free and flowing with good drive and a straight action from front to rear. He should retain a level topline and carry his head in a proud and dignified manner, displaying character and confidence. His movement should give the impression that he is happy and really enjoying his parading in the show ring; any jerkiness or awkward movement of limbs will detract from the dog's performance. In order to ensure a good movement and a graceful gait it is essential that the puppy receives plenty of exercise and that he is well trained for the show ring. Any lack of confidence in the show ring will be apparent in the dog's movement and will be evident to the judge.

Coat, Colour and Texture

The colour of the Yorkshire Terrier is a very important feature of the breed, the combination of steel blue and golden-shaded tan appearing only in the Yorkshire Terrier and in its Australian cousin, the Silky.

The steel blue varies from dark steel through to a light medium blue. The optimum colour is somewhere in between. It should not be jet black or a washed-out pale silver, although these colours do occur. The steel blue of the body should be as even as possible. The colour break usually starts on the top of the neck of puppies at about four months of age, but it can start earlier and still finish a good medium blue. The other correct type of colour break is an all-over break, which can also take place at about four months.

The definition of the word 'tan', used in the Breed Standards has, for many years, caused confusion. The colour should be similar to the gold of a 22-carat wedding ring, not to the colour of a pair of tan shoes or a tan shirt. Newcomers to the breed still seem to misunder-

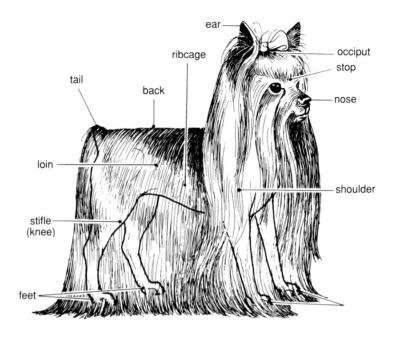

The Yorkshire Terrier: areas of the body.

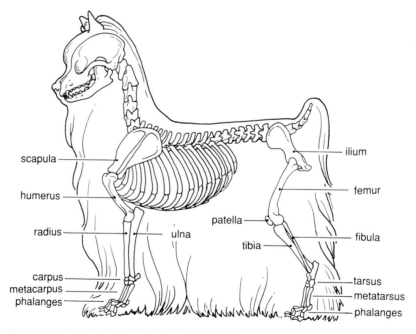

The Yorkshire Terrier: the major bones in the body.

70

roach back

down at shoulder

correct back

Diagrams showing correct and incorrect toplines.

stand what is required. The gold should be deeper at the roots, shading to a lighter colour at the tips. It is hard to explain, but once seen on a beautiful specimen of the breed, it is never forgotten.

The steel blue is less easy to describe because steel does come in different colours, but if you break open a piece of coke the colour inside is metallic blue-grey with absolutely no hint of any other

semi-erect

flop or drop ear

correct

too large

wide set

Ear carriage: correct and incorrect placement.

colour. In a show dog, there should never be a brownish or yellowish tinge to the blue.

Jet black dogs have no place in the show ring or in a breeding programme, no matter how good they happen to be in other respects, whereas a light bitch can play an important role when mated to a good-coloured dog, often throwing a proportion of good-coloured puppies. The correct coat texture is heavy and silken, with every hair straight and separate. It should never be dull like cotton wool or profuse like a brush. It should shine with health and both colours should have a metallic gleam to them.

Size

To conform to the Kennel Club's Breed Standard the Yorkshire Terrier must not weigh more than 7 pounds (3.1kg). Although most young adult Yorkshire Terriers would be well within this limit, it is important that they should not be allowed to eat to excess as they grow older so making them fat and affecting their health.

Though the Yorkshire Terrier has his origins firmly placed in Britain, he has over the years been enthusiastically embraced by dog fanciers the world over, nowhere more so than in the United States of America.
    Early American breeders and exhibitors were working with a variety of different guide-lines until a common Standard was accepted by the American Kennel Club in 1912. This was the Breed Standard in use in the United Kingdom at that time and remained in use until 1966. So for more than half a century breeders both sides of the Atlantic were working to exactly the same Breed Standard, though the emphasis given to certain aspects of the breed's development differed. The current Standard was drawn up by the Yorkshire Terrier Club of America and then approved by the American Kennel Club in 1966. Generally there are very few differences between the American and British Standards, if anything the main differences have been in emphasis and interpretation. In 1989, I had the privilege to judge the Delaware Valley Yorkshire Terrier Club Championship Show and found that while the American breeders had worked exceedingly hard on the Yorkshire Terrier's soundness, and produced exhibits with good movement, they had not striven to produce the same coat quality that exists in Britain.

The American Breed Standard

(Reproduced by kind permission of the American Kennel Club)

General Appearance

That of a long-haired toy terrier whose blue and tan coat is parted on the face and from the base of the skull to the end of the tail and hangs evenly and quite straight down each side of body. The body is neat, compact and well proportioned. The dog's high head carriage and confident manner should give the appearance of vigor and self-importance.

Head

Small and rather flat on top, *the skull* not too prominent or round, *the muzzle* not too long, with *the bite* neither undershot nor overhsot and teeth sound. Either scissors bite or level bite is acceptable. *The nose* is black. *Eyes* are medium in size and not too prominent; dark in color and sparkling with a sharp, intelligent expression. Eye rims are dark. *Ears* are small, V-shaped, carried erect and set not too far apart.

Body

Well proportioned and very compact. The back is rather short, the back line level, with height at shoulder the same as at the rump.

Legs and Feet

Forelegs should be straight, elbows neither in nor out. *Hind legs* straight when viewed from behind, but stifles are moderately bent when viewed from the sides. *Feet* are found with black toenails. Dewclaws, if any, are generally removed from the hind legs. Dewclaws on the forelegs may be removed.

Tail

Docked to a medium length and carried slightly higher than the level of the back.

Coat

Quality, texture and quantity of coat are of prime importance. Hair is glossy, fine and silky in texture. Coat on the body is moderately long and perfectly straight (not wavy). It may be trimmed to floor length to give ease of movement and a neater appearance, if desired. The fall on the head is long, tied with one bow in center of head or parted in the middle and tied with two bows. Hair on muzzle is very long. Hair should be trimmed short on tips of ears and may be trimmed on feet to give them a neat appearance.

Colors

Puppies are born black and tan and are normally darker in body color, showing an intermingling of black hair in the tan until they are matured. Color of hair on body and richness of tan on head and legs are of prime importance in *adult dogs*, to which the following colour requirements apply:

Blue Is a dark-steel-blue, not a silver-blue and not mingled with fawn, bronzy or black hairs.

Tan All tan hair is darker at the roots than in the middle, shading to still lighter tan at the tips. There should be no sooty or black hair intermingled with any of the tan.

Color on Body

The blue extends over the body from back of neck to root of tail. Hair on tail is a darker blue, especially at end of tail.

Headfall

A rich golden tan, deeper in color at sides of head, at ear roots and on the muzzle, with ears a deep rich tan. Tan color should not extend down on back of neck.

Chest and Legs

A bright, rich tan, not extending above the elbow on the forelegs nor above the stifle on hind legs.

Weight

Must not exceed seven pounds.

3

Buying a Yorkshire Terrier

Popularity of the Breed

The Yorkshire Terrier has become one of the world's most popular breeds in modern times. This is undoubtedly because of his size, looks and adorable personality; owners have moulded the character of their dogs into little people.

Owing to their size, Yorkshire Terriers need very limited exercise and eat very little, making them economical to keep and maintain. Furthermore, they need only a very small living space which makes them ideal for people living and working in towns and cities. One of the most exciting aspects of this breed is the glamorous coat and colouring. Although the breed is equally at home in the town or enjoying the freedom of the open countryside, the Yorkshire Terrier living in the country should have his coat shortened by regular trimming. As a Yorkshire Terrier never moults, life will be more comfortable with a shorter and more easily managed coat.

A Yorkshire Terrier, because of his size, makes an ideal travelling companion and although they love walking, they will exercise themselves in small spaces when necessary.

Yorkshire Terriers are a comparatively long-lived breed and so make good, faithful long-term friends; it is not uncommon for them to reach fifteen years of age.

Finally, they have become one of the most popular breeds in the show arena and so offer a great potential and opportunity to the owner who is interested in entering the show world.

Responsibilities of Ownership

The decision to buy a Yorkshire Terrier puppy, or any other breed, should not be taken lightly. The potential owner must be aware that

*Actress Bette Davis
with her much-loved pet,
Ozmilion Thomas.*

he is taking on a variety of responsibilities. These will be briefly outlined in the following paragraphs and expanded upon in later chapters.

As a dog owner, you will have a responsibility for your dog and also for your dog's actions. Being responsible for your dog means providing the love, care and facilities to see that he has a healthy and happy life. This will include such aspects as providing him with bedding and housing and seeing that he is comfortable and has enough space to develop. You must also see that he has a healthy diet, is fed regularly and that he receives all the nutritional supplements he needs. A very important aspect of this responsibility will involve ensuring that he gets all the necessary vaccinations, nursing when ill and a generally healthy active lifestyle with enough exercise and play to keep him happy. Most importantly you must provide much love and companionship as this is extremely important for his character development. Also very important with a Yorkshire Terrier is the care of his coat and appearance; keeping his coat in excellent condition will require some effort on your behalf. Only if you have the time available to cater for all these needs should you consider owning a Yorkshire Terrier; to acquire one without being able to give him the love and attention he needs would be most unfair to the dog.

Being responsible for the actions of your pet means your responsibility to other people and animals with whom he will interact. As an owner you are responsible for ensuring that your puppy does not cause inconvenience to others. Generally this includes preventing such nuisance as excessive barking, running loose, fouling the pavement and being left to howl when shut up. Try to avoid allowing your dog's behaviour to become a source of annoyance to others. It is your social responsibility to make sure that your puppy does not foul the pavement or other public places. Make sure that you carry a small plastic bag or something similar to clean up any accidents that may occur when exercising him.

Problems of Ownership

Most of the problems associated with owning a Yorkshire Terrier puppy are to be found in the home as the puppy is unlikely to leave this environment for the first sixteen weeks of his life. Children may prove to be a source of problems; this is only natural as the puppy is so small and fragile at this stage. When children are around and the puppy is loose, the owner should stay close at hand to help prevent any unforeseen accidents such as the puppy being dropped and sustaining damage to his limbs. This would be bad enough in a pet but could prove a disaster in a potential show dog as the dog's movement may be impaired. Similar damage could be caused by falling over or on the puppy or accidentally kicking or dropping something on him. Adults must also be aware of the puppy being loose around their feet as they can cause equally if not more serious damage to the puppy, who will probably weigh only 1½ pounds (0.7kg).

The average home contains many serious hazards to the Yorkshire Terrier puppy. As the puppy is so close to the floor he has easy access to electrical wires and plugs. It is in the puppy's nature to chew things and, should he accidentally chew through a live wire, the consequences could be fatal to him, let alone the danger of an electrical fire with all of the associated damage to the home or even loss of human life.

You must also be prepared for the effect that a new puppy may have on your other family pets. The puppy may enter your home having had no contact with other animals apart from his mother or

Author's sister Zakia Collins with the young Ozmilion Wild Mink and Ozmilion Personality.

other puppies. The consequences of a boisterous and over-friendly puppy disturbing the sleeping family cat in its own territory can easily be imagined, so you must be vigilant to ensure that problems do not arise.

Choices to Make

When a decision has been made to purchase a Yorkshire Terrier the potential owner is still left with a number of important choices, whether to have an adult dog or puppy, a dog or a bitch, a show dog or a pet.

Adult Dog or Puppy?

Either choice will have its own advantages and disadvantages. To some, choosing and buying a puppy and the work and devotion needed to nurture this tiny animal through all the growing problems, training and character development that will bring it to adulthood, are a major part of the joy of ownership. The Yorkshire Terrier is classed as a puppy until he is twelve months old, by which stage he

Ozmilion Clarence, 3lb in weight, the author's much-loved family pet, a son of Int. Ch. Ozmilion Jubilation.

will have most of his adult teeth, be house-trained and vaccinated. Therefore an adult dog may be a much better choice for buyers such as elderly couples and young families who may not have the time or ability to take on the responsibility of bringing up and caring for a puppy. If you do decide to buy a puppy do try to see the mother and father of the potential choice to assess the temperament as no one wants a puppy who will turn snappy in adulthood.

To decide to keep and run on a puppy is quite a big decision in itself, because you could be wrong and then the little dog will later have to go to a new home at an older age when it is not so easy for him to settle. However, Yorkshire Terriers are such great characters and so lovable at any age that there is usually someone nice just waiting to give them a loving permanent home. If there is not a suitable home immediately it should not be too long before the right person comes along. In other instances this right person could just be you, having decided to opt for the more mature adult dog.

Show Dog or Pet?

It is important at the outset to have a clear idea of your reasons for keeping the dog. A Yorkshire Terrier bought solely as a pet need not be so carefully selected as one for show, but care should be taken that the dog or pup is healthy, sound and of a good temperament. Having said this many new owners of pet dogs become so enchanted with them that they start to show them. The purchase of a dog primarily for show use requires considerable care and research. Time spent reading relevant books, visiting dog shows and gathering informa-

*Baroness Marina v Bernus's much-adored pet Ozmilion My
Attraction at 1 year old.*

tion will never be wasted. Many breeders will be of great assistance
to you in your search for the correct animal, but beware of the rogues
who exist in the breeding world just as in any other. If you do get
caught out, it is likely that you did not do a thorough enough job of
research in the first place.

An important part of the selection process is a visit to the breeder
to check on the blood-line you wish to buy. Carefully observe the
parents of the potential purchase in their own environment. The
mother should be happy, have a nice temperament and will probably
approach you with tail wagging; the father should have the same
traits. Look also for that bright character needed in the show ring.
Remember that the puppy from an ill-tempered mother and father
could well prove snappy in adulthood and therefore be a bad choice.

Dog or Bitch?

The best choice for show purposes is probably a bitch, as you can
then breed from her at a later date if she is big enough. If she is a good
bitch then you should show her, get the experience and enjoyment

Mr and Mrs T. Priest's young male Presquin Millionaire.

from showing and then mate her with a compatible dog to get your-self a puppy which you can train and develop for show. Showing a puppy which you have bred yourself can be a great thrill. Get the best quality bitch that you can afford; if she is not of the best quality, do not show her as she will not be successful.

Should you, on the other hand, choose to buy a male, make sure that he is the best show-quality dog you can afford. If he is successful at show and of good line and temperament, then you can use him as a stud-dog. You will be able to buy a puppy from this mating and can charge a stud fee. There is of course no perfect dog or bitch but the fewer faults in the chosen animal, the better.

When you finally go to look for your new dog you should have a good idea of exactly what you are looking for, but do be realistic when going to view dogs. A top breeder is not going to sell you a potential record-breaking champion at the cost of an average pet dog. You should have a good idea of the current market price for the quality of dog you seek, having done all the initial research such as reading, and talking to knowledgeable people. Having made your choices between puppy or adult, dog or bitch, and pet or show dog, you now know what you are looking for. With this in mind you should consider where to look for your future friend.

Where to Buy your Puppy

Although there are many different sources from which you could purchase your Yorkshire Terrier puppy, not all can be recommended. Without doubt the best place to buy your pedigree puppy is from a specialist Yorkshire Terrier breeder who has regularly produced good stock and where the relatives of the puppy can be seen.

The Kennel Club will supply you with a list of reputable breeders in your area or you can buy the *Kennel Gazette*, their official publication, which gives lists of breeders for each breed. There is usually quite a good list of Yorkshire Terrier breeders. If the puppy is bought from a reliable breeder, it is most likely to be healthy and in good condition. This is not always the case when buying from dealers who buy in litters of puppies for resale, and who do not understand Yorkshire Terriers as well as the specialist breeder. There are some kennels that are well run, but as their proprietors usually buy in stock from breeders, some are much better reared than others, and all are going to be sold at a profit over and above their original price, so your new puppy could be unnecessarily expensive. Apart from this, the risks of infection are increased whenever there is a constant coming and going of puppies.

You may see puppies advertised in a local paper or in your local vet's or pet shop's windows. Great care has to be taken when purchasing through such sources as it may reflect the lack of experience of the breeder and be reflected in the puppies' development. Be especially wary of any advertisements that say 'can' or 'will' deliver as this is not a way that a reputable breeder would advertise.

Buying an Adult Dog

Should you have decided to purchase an adult dog instead of a puppy then there are one or two other places you may look in the search for your new dog. However, it is still recommended that you

Mr J. Magri's Rozamie Careless Whisper, aged 1 year, dam to Ch. Rozamie Endless Love.

contact established breeders as they may have a dog that is suitable for you or may be able to put you in personal contact with someone who has.

If you are looking for a pet, you may be lucky and find your perfect companion at a local dog rescue as they do have Yorkshire Terriers from time to time. It may well be worth your while to check for a Yorkshire Terrier Rescue in your area, the address of which you can get from the Kennel Club. Dogs can end up in dog rescues for many reasons and not necessarily because they have been mistreated or abandoned, so it is possible to find a well-adjusted, bright and perfectly healthy dog. While you are visiting, be sure to learn as much as possible of the background to any dog you have taken a shine to; the kennel staff should be able to help you here, particularly if you visit a rescue for a specialist breed as the staff will be good judges of the dogs' characters and able to say if one is likely to suit your own environment. Some owners can have genuine reasons for having to part with their loved companions, such as a change in lifestyle, a move to a different environment, ill health or a new member of the family to cater for. These people will sometimes advertise locally and may insist on a good home for their pet to go to, so do not take offence if they interview you when you come to see the dog, as this will show that they do care about what will happen to their old friend and also be a sign that the dog has been well cared for. It is the owners who 'can't get rid of it quickly enough' and who ask you little about your own environment that you should be most wary of.

If you are looking for a dog to breed from or to show in the show ring then it is unlikely that you will find what you need outside of the specialist breeder and the show world. Only by visiting breeders and dog shows and keeping your eyes on the specialist dog press are you going to find animals suitable for your requirements.

What to Look For

When you arrive to view any dogs as a prospective buyer it is important that you should be completely open and honest about the dog's future. If it is a show dog you are looking for, then say so. The breeder will know his dogs well and is more likely to know of any faults the puppy may have that would hinder him as a show dog when he matures. The breeder can only help you get what you want if you tell him exactly why you want the dog and what you expect of him. This honesty should be reciprocated; any good breeder who is proud of his dogs should only sell to you if he can meet your requirements and not be looking to offload his stock on to the next person through his door. This is one good reason why a recommended breeder with a good reputation should be your first choice.

Do not buy a dog without having seen him first. This sounds common sense, but often people negotiate by telephone or letter and sometimes everything is quite satisfactory, but there is nothing like seeing a dog for yourself. Arrange to visit the breeder even if it is a long way off. Hopefully you will see a litter of friendly, healthy puppies with their mother. The opposite to this is a litter of timid little creatures with dull staring eyes who do not want to come out of their box. Sad as this may be, do not buy one because you feel sorry for him. You could be buying a lot of trouble for you and your family which might well involve expensive vet's fees.

The Yorkshire Terrier's eyes should be bright and clean and free from any mucus discharge. Their eyes do water, particularly while they are teething and a little 'sleep' can remain in the corners of their eyes. However, anything resembling yellow or greenish matter is definitely suspect and should be avoided.

Ears may be up, or down because of teething, and this is not detrimental under five months of age, but they should not have any strong odour coming from inside the ear, as this could indicate ear

Mr and Mrs M. Dawson's Ch. Mondamin My Minstrel at the age of 8 months.

mites. This can be remedied by a trip to the vet, but it must be done immediately or the mites could be passed on to any other dogs you may own. If their kennel has been soiled, any motion should be a medium brown in colour and well formed. The stool varies according to diet and is usually softer when they are given a milky feed rather than solid food. This must not be confused with diarrhoea, which is very loose, usually has a pungent smell and sometimes has blood in it. Avoid puppies with diarrhoea at all costs.

Ask to see the puppies on the ground if the breeder carries them to you. Do not choose the smallest, most backward puppy, as there could be a reason for his slow development. If it is not just as good on its legs and as lively as the rest it is better not to take it. When handling the puppy there should be no signs of deformed ligaments. If in doubt, ask the breeder.

Good breeders take great pains to produce top-quality, sound stock and in the process get extremely attached to their dogs. Do not be surprised to be closely questioned about the life your little dog will lead and such things as housing conditions, secure fencing round the garden and so forth. Breeders will not let puppies go unless they feel fully confident that they will receive the same loving care in their new homes. Just because you have paid for your puppy and it has now become your property does not mean the breeder has no right to know of your puppy's progress. Keep in touch without being a nusiance. Most dog breeders are very busy people but do like to hear of their stock's progress from time to time – not necessarily every week as some over-enthusiastic new owners seem to think. You would not have your Yorkshire Terrier if it were not for the breeder and so some contact is appreciated. After all, it may not be all that long before you decide you want another.

Buying your Show Puppy

Before you decide to purchase a show puppy a great deal of thought should be given to your selection. Read as much as possible: magazines such as *Our Dogs, Dog World* and *Dogs Monthly* are ideal for background information and can put you in contact with specialist breeders. It is a good idea to visit dog shows and speak to exhibitors; most breeders will be only too happy to give you any information you may require. Do not make any hasty decisions. If you are lucky enough to live near a reputable specialist breeder and can visit, so much the better. Study the different strains and try to picture the type that would most please you.

With this decision made, care should be taken to examine the puppy carefully. Besides bearing in mind all the advice about choosing a pet puppy given in the earlier section and being familiar with the current Breed Standard, there are a few other aspects to be considered when looking for that special puppy. Here is a guide to what the puppy should possess, remembering that the perfect dog has not yet been born. A puppy should appear to be intelligent, fearless, loving, interested and willing to please. Sometimes a slightly shy puppy can be brought out of itself but it is better if it is outgoing in the first place.

Conformation

Look for a level topline with correct tail placement, tail carried slightly higher than the level of the back. Often a very showy puppy has a 'gay' tail at home but by the time it gets to the show ring, it does not carry it so high.

The puppy should have the correct length of back in proportion to height, giving the body a square appearance. Remember short legs do not usually move with the drive required and are often hopeless trying to move through grass at outdoor shows. If the legs are too long, the puppy looks like it is on stilts and again is out of proportion. The correct reach of neck is medium length flowing into well-formed shoulders. The front legs should be straight when viewed from the front. The shoulders should fit in well with no suggestion of out-turned elbows. The rear should again be a happy medium, not too angular nor too straight, giving a stiff appearance.

Assess the puppy's movement. He must be able to move freely without exaggeration but with drive from behind. The head should be refined with neat, well-placed ears, as dark an eye as possible and dense black pigmentation on the nose. There should be promise of an abundant coat of clear colours. In an extra special puppy there should be other refinements that outclass its contemporaries.

Age

Ideally, dogs bought as show specimens should be purchased as near to six months as possible but one must remember that even at this age they may fail to mature to the breeder's or your own high expectations. With puppies much younger than six months it is much harder to predict a dog's development and so it is quite a risk when choosing such a young puppy for its show potential. Because of this no quality breeder will guarantee that a puppy will be suitable for showing or breeding as it matures. As a puppy matures and develops into a good show dog its value will increase making it a more expensive purchase and a better bet for the future, but it may be the more prudent purchase as a lot of money could be wasted on younger dogs who fail to develop into good show examples.

The Formalities

Having found the puppy or dog you want and agreed the price, there are still a couple of things you need to be aware of. Firstly, be sure to ask for and get a receipt for the purchase. If you are buying a pedigree dog be sure you receive a copy of the pedigree; this is a record of your puppy's blood-line, usually spanning four or five generations. This is an indication of blood-lines, which you will need

Liz and Tom Putman's 10-week-old puppy, Tomlizan Love Creation.

should you use the puppy for showing or breeding. In addition, you should receive from the breeder a Kennel Club Registration Certificate for your dog. This will state your puppy's name, Kennel Club registration number and brief details of parentage. This Registration Certificate should be sent to the Kennel Club along with the necessary fee so that you can be registered as the new owner.

Check with the breeder that the puppy's course of vaccinations has been completed and ask for a vet's certificate to confirm this. If the vaccinations have not been completed, then be sure to arrange this yourself with your own local vet before leaving with your new puppy. You should ask the breeder for a diet sheet and any other information he can give on your puppy's feeding habits; this way you can keep to the same feeding regime as any sudden changes could upset the puppy's stomach. You should also ask the breeder for the date the puppy was last wormed. It is also advisable to get your vet to check the new puppy thoroughly as soon as possible so both you and the breeder are satisfied with the transaction and there are no problems.

4

Care and Management

Care of the Puppy

In the last chapter we talked about acquiring a puppy and touched on the responsibilities of dog ownership in general. In this chapter we will explore in more detail what exactly is required in the day-to-day care of this wonderful little animal, the Yorkshire Terrier puppy.

Just like humans, the puppy has many needs which we, as responsible owners, must cater for. The most basic needs are for food and shelter, but to cater for these two needs alone is far from sufficient. Having chosen a Yorkshire Terrier, we have a responsibility to see that he remains healthy, keeps clean and develops the sparkling personality he is capable of. To achieve this you must be able to devote a fair amount of time and certainly lots of love and attention to your new friend. This is particularly important from such a young age as this is when the dog's character is going to be formed. There is certainly some truth in the old adage 'you can't teach an old dog new tricks'; it is in the early days that you have the opportunity to encourage in your dog the endearing personality that is so well known in the breed. By taking good care of your puppy, it will repay you many times over with its love and loyalty and give you endless hours of joy.

Before collecting the puppy you will need to visit your local pet shop. The following is a list of items that you will require:

Lead   Bedding
Puppy collar   Toilet trainers
Feeding bowls   Vitamin supplements
Toys   Pure bristle brush
Chews   Metal comb
Bed   Shampoo

Although this list may seem long to the novice owner it is not really daunting as many of the items should be a once and forever purchase if you choose a reasonable quality to begin with. There is a vast range of products and accessories available to the dog owner. Your puppy's breeder may be able to advise you on which ones to purchase, and a good pet shop will also be able to help you.

Bedding should be safe and, ideally, washable. When choosing toys, make sure that you select only those that are made of a hard material to avoid the puppy chewing pieces off and possibly choking itself. Care should also be taken when buying vitamin supplements. It would be wise to seek the guidance of your vet or the breeder.

A good lead for the Yorkshire Terrier puppy is the light show type as this will be easier for him to adjust to at first. Before taking the puppy outside on the lead for the first time it is useful to get it accustomed to walking with the lead indoors first. To begin with about ten minutes a day should be devoted to this. Let the puppy go wherever it wants and lead you around; later you can lead the puppy around, getting down to its level to give encouragement where needed. Most puppies will probably follow your feet at first anyway, making your initial task easier.

Socializing

Small puppies need to socialize with humans as well as with other dogs, as this helps to develop their characters. Be careful not to allow strangers to make too much fuss, and encourage them to play with the puppy on the floor to avoid too much picking up. Great care should be taken when small children are around as children can become boisterous in play and may injure the puppy, who will be quite small and fragile at this stage.

Health of your Puppy

Dogs, just like humans, are prone to many kinds of infections and illnesses. It is therefore important to protect your dog where possible and to be able to recognize when your dog is ill and what action to take. There are many aspects of your dog's health that you can take care of yourself but there are times when the services of your local veterinary surgeon will be required. It is important to keep your vet's address and telephone number to hand just in case your dog becomes suddenly ill and needs urgent attention.

The more common complaints that your dog may acquire are discussed in the later chapter on ailments and diseases (*see* page 164). Should you be worried about any aspect of your dog's health and do not know what to do, then you must seek advice from your local vet, just as you yourself would see a doctor when you do not know what is wrong with you.

There are a number of viral infections that dogs are particularly prone to and which can have serious if not fatal consequences should your dog contract them. The most common viruses are distemper, hepatitis, leptospirosis and parvovirus.

Fortunately, we can now protect our dogs from these viruses with a course of vaccinations.

Vaccinations

Your initial concern will be to see that your puppy is protected against those dangerous diseases from which he is at risk. This will involve getting your vet to administer a course of vaccinations.

When a puppy is born the mother passes antibodies to it through her milk. These antibodies will help to protect the puppy against most infectious diseases, including distemper, hepatitis, leptospirosis and parvovirus. These, however, are not permanent and become ineffective after a period of time which can vary from between just a few days to around fourteen weeks. Therefore, it can be seen that the timing of the puppy's first vaccination can also be varied and usually occurs between five and eight weeks after birth. The timing often depends on the environment from which the puppy comes: a puppy coming from a healthy environment would probably have its first vaccinations at eight to nine weeks, whereas one from a suspect environment, where there may be a higher risk of disease, would have its vaccinations earlier.

After the first vaccination the vet will advise you when the second and third vaccinations are due. Usually these are two and four weeks respectively after the first vaccinations. Once this course of injections is completed your puppy will be protected against many of the common diseases, and is safe to go outside and mix with other animals and people.

In order to continue protection for your dog it is necessary to see that the dog has regular boosters each year. The booster injections give cover for all of the viruses at one go rather than in a series as the initial injections are.

Worming

When you visit the vet's surgery for vaccinations he should ask you if the puppy has been wormed. If it has not he will provide you with the correct medication and instructions on how to administer it.

Sleeping Arrangements

There are a few aspects to be considered in providing some kind of sleeping arrangement for your puppy or dog. The most obvious is how much room you have in your home that could be used for your pet. This is not usually a problem if it is your sole animal as it can fit in around you, provided that some care is taken. But if you own a few dogs and/or other animals, then more thought is going to be required if you are going to manage them properly, and kennels should be considered.

At first the puppy will feel disorientated in his new surroundings. He will also probably feel very lonely being separated from his mother and brothers and sisters. He will probably cry at night and this may be helped by wrapping a hot water bottle in some bedding to simulate his mothers warmth. The sound of a radio playing softly or even a ticking clock will soothe him and help him sleep.

In order to make your new puppy feel secure it is important that it is given its own special place to sleep, a place it can mark with its own scent and consider its own. Initially, a cardboard box can be used, cut down at the front so the puppy can get in and out. Although the puppy will tend to chew on the box this can easily be replaced as often as necessary. Your puppy should be given something soft to sleep on, such as an old blanket, cushion or specially purchased vet bed. As the puppy grows you could replace the cardboard boxes with a dog basket or with a kennel. Although they are more attractive it is not advisable to have a wicker basket for a growing puppy as puppies will chew at anything they can get their teeth into, and the wicker splinters very easily and could be swallowed, causing problems.

Whichever accommodation you provide for your puppy you must consider where is the best place to site it. This should be somewhere that is safe, out of harm's way, warm and not in a draught.

One excellent way of producing further security for your puppy is to make or buy him a puppy-pen. These are very useful and most can

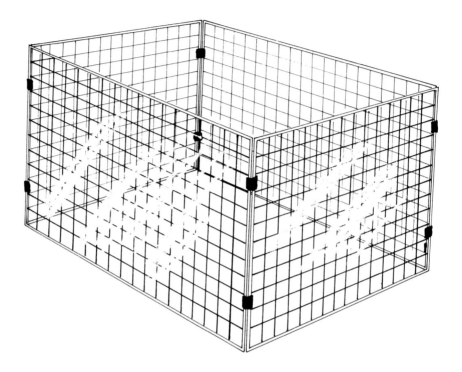

Wire-mesh puppy pen.

be folded up and stored away when not in use. The puppy-pen should be made of square wire mesh so that you can always see your dog and he can see you too; this is particularly important with a breed like the Yorkshire which possesses such curiosity. Be sure that the size of mesh is too small for the puppy to get his head through as he may become trapped or injured if he can squeeze through the mesh. Also the pen's sides should be high enough to prevent the puppy climbing out; if the pen is too low the puppy may try to jump or climb out and could well sustain serious injuries in his attempts. There should be plenty of room in the pen for the puppy's bedding, the rest of the floor space can then be covered with newspapers.

Besides securing the puppy out of harm's way these pens have many other uses, particularly so when you have a few dogs to manage at the same time. These pens are ideal for isolating a mother and her litter from other dogs; also for a show dog who is growing his coat and needs to be isolated from other dogs and obstacles that could ruin it. Besides keeping your puppy out of mischief a pen can assist in disciplining your dog, so aiding his training and possible introduction to the show world.

Kennels

Yorkshire Terriers should always be kennelled indoors, as they love to be close to their owners and need constant love and attention. Because of their size and endearing character there can be no excuse for not keeping them in excellent condition at all times.

If a number of dogs are to be kept at any one time, a separate room should be set aside for them. This room should be kept at a constant 60°F (15.5°C) and be well ventilated. In many houses the kitchen will have to serve dual purpose and will work provided that there are not too many dogs and that there is sufficient room for them not to get in the way at busy times, when some form of kennel will be needed for each dog. These can be of a proprietary brand or purpose built. The interior of the kennels should be easy to clean and the floor area kept

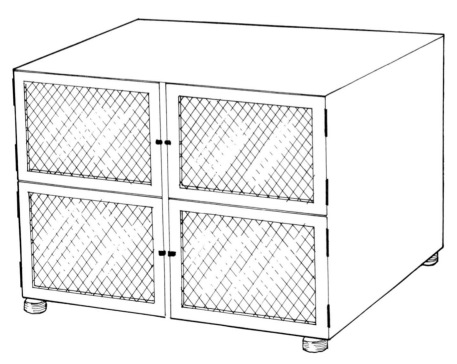

Indoor kennels.

lined with plenty of dry, clean newspaper. Bedding can be either proprietary dog beds or suitable blankets which need to be changed daily. Blankets or beds with holes or which are fraying are dangerous to small dogs and must be avoided.

Whilst this sort of accommodation is excellent for sleeping, the Yorkshire Terrier is a lively active dog during the day and should be running about in the garden, or indoors during wet weather. The dogs will be much happier if they are allowed to run around with the least possible restriction during the day. If the dogs have to be kept in a run in the garden ensure that this is kept clean and dry, preferably under cover and shaded from direct sunlight. It is a good idea to have some old bedding and some familiar items in the run for the dogs to play with.

When you have a number of dogs to look after, kennels are essential for many reasons. Each dog should have his own place and bed, the dogs can be separated when feeding so as to ensure that each one gets his own meal. At times it may be necessary to isolate one or more dogs for various reasons such as injury or illness, to keep dogs away from bitches or to protect a show dog's coat. Ideally each dog should have his own kennel and this should not be cramped. A kennel compartment of a reasonable size for a Yorkshire Terrier would be 24 inches wide, 24 inches deep and 18 inches high (60 × 60 × 45cm). Obviously how many kennels you have will be determined by the number of dogs you have and the space you have available at your home. Whether you buy or build your own kennels there are a few features that are essential. There must be a mesh front to allow fresh air in, ideally ½ inch (1cm) wire mesh, and a secure catch that cannot be opened from the inside by your dog. Also the kennels must be easy to clean and at a convenient height for you to manage.

House-Training

An important aspect of owning a puppy is that it has to be house-trained, which will keep both your home and the puppy clean. Young puppies will not soil their own beds, but will go anywhere else in the house to relieve themselves. If you give them their own spot with some newspapers and train them to go to that spot and nowhere else in the room, this will be more hygienic and comfortable for both you and your puppy. You should decide the best place for the puppy to be trained to use. A corner is usually best as it is easier to keep your puppy in the corner while he uses the paper. In order to encourage your dog to use the newspaper you can buy a liquid or spray from your local pet shop, which has an odour which attracts the puppy. A puppy will give tell-tale signs when it needs to go. It will sniff around the floor when it wants to urinate, or walk around in circles with its head low to the floor when it wishes to empty its bowels. This will be the signal to put your puppy on the newspaper and stay with it, so that it cannot move away from the newspaper you have sprayed. Giving it lots of encouragement to go is helpful and when it has finished, give the puppy lots of praise so that it knows you are pleased with it. Using the newspaper method you should have a well-trained, clean puppy within a reasonable time.

During this training period there may be the odd accident, so if you can keep the puppy on a tiled or linoleum floor it will make life much easier for you. If your puppy does have an accident on your carpet there are various products available from your pet shop which can be used to clean the carpet; a puppy only urinates a small quantity so you may find a little disinfectant and some tissue will be adequate.

Never rub your puppy's nose in his toilet as this is ineffective, very unhygienic, and could cause infestation of worms. Until your puppy is completely vaccinated he should be kept inside your home and not even allowed out into the garden as this would put him at risk from disease. Once the puppy's vaccinations have been completed and the vet clears him to venture outside it is time to go to the toilet outside when possible. The ideal place would be the garden or, if in a flat, a balcony is ideal but be sure that the puppy will not fall through the railings. Generally puppies should be put out first thing in the morning and then again at frequent intervals throughout the day, especially after meals. Initially it is a good idea to stay with your puppy so as to encourage it when he actually goes. This way it will learn where is the right place to go. When you eventually take your puppy out in public you are responsible for its actions. Do not allow it to foul the footpath as this is unpleasant to other footpath users and, if caught, you will be liable for a fine.

When your dog does need to relieve himself make him use the gutter and do clear up after him. Fortunately, with a Yorkshire Terrier, there is never a lot of mess to clear up and this is easily done with a poop-scoop which is available from pet shops. Alternatively, you can use a little scoop and a plastic bag. You can either take this rubbish home with you or wrap it in a bag and dispose of it in a nearby rubbish bin.

Teething

The Yorkshire Terrier is quite prone to dental problems, most of which occur during the young dog's teething period which can be just as troublesome as that of the human baby. A puppy will start to cut his teeth at around three to four weeks, with the second set through by the time he reaches eight or nine months of age. The full set of teeth in the upper jaw consists of six incisors, two canines, eight premolars and four molars making a total of twenty teeth. The lower jaw carries twenty-two teeth and mirrors the upper set with the exception of having three molars on each side, one more than the upper jaw. This gives a full mouth of forty-two teeth.

Two rows of teeth may often be apparent during the teething process. If this happens and the first teeth are loose you may be able to work them free with your fingers. If you are not able to do this with ease, it would be wise to consult the veterinary surgeon who may have to remove the milk teeth. It is important to check all dogs with their adult teeth for double canines; this occurs when the first canine remains in the gum during teething and is apparent as a small curved tooth lodged behind the adult canine. If left in place this tooth will encourage the development of plaque and gum disease which will lead to loss of the adult canine, therefore the milk canine must be removed by the veterinary surgeon.

Failure to look after the dog's teeth will lead to problems such as tartar build-up and bad breath, and eventually to gum disease which causes the gums to recede in adult dogs with subsequent loosening and loss of teeth. Bad teeth and gums can also bring about digestive disorders and lack of appetite, with some dogs refusing to eat at all. Painful teeth and gum infections can also lead to ill-tempered, snappy dogs and other behavioural problems. Young puppies often have gum problems which become apparent as red and swollen tissue. Often this interferes with the teeth breaking through and even prevents the ears from becoming erect.

Giving the puppies marrow and chew bones will relieve painful gums and encourage the teeth to emerge, but take care not to give very small bones or any that may splinter. Adult dogs should also be encouraged to chew as this will reduce plaque and strengthen the gums. However, a show dog should not be given bones or chews as this practice will cause him to damage the facial moustaches. A good substitute in this case would be hard biscuits. Once the dog is retired from showing he should, of course, be encouraged to chew bones as

Joe Magri's 8-week-old puppy, Rozamie Hamlet.

this will maintain the health of his teeth and gums. The adult dog's teeth should also be cleaned by the owner using a child's toothbrush and an appropriate toothpaste. Where heavy deposits of plaque are apparent it will be necessary to visit the vet to have the dog's teeth descaled. If care is taken during the teething period and maintained throughout early life problems with the dog's teeth in later years can be minimized.

Puppy Feeding

Puppies adapt very easily and quickly from being fed by their mother to feeding themselves, although at the beginning they may be a little clumsy and messy. At first it is best to use a solid heavy bowl that cannot be moved around easily by the puppy. Ideally this bowl should be shallow with a raised rim to stop it stepping into its food and treading it around as well as clogging its paws. Also it is best to designate one spot in which to feed the puppy as it will become familiar with this place; it should be a safe place for the puppy and out of danger of people walking over it. When you have two or more puppies or dogs feeding it is important to see that each gets its share of food. If there is a greedy member in the group you will have to separate them at their feeding times to ensure they each get the correct amount of food, neither too much nor too little.

If you did not breed the puppy yourself then when you first receive your puppy it is important to adhere as closely as possible to the breeder's diet sheet so as not to upset the puppy's stomach. Any changes to this diet should be introduced gradually so that the puppy will get used to the new food. There are many different types of food that are suitable for a puppy but care must be taken to ensure that it gets all the nourishment it needs during this important growing period. A typical feeding schedule would be as follows:

Diet Sheet

Weaning to six weeks old

After the puppy has been weaned, usually from three weeks old, he should receive four meals a day.

Breakfast This should consist of approximately one tablespoonful of baby cereal or rusk, or a complete pre-prepared puppy food which can be fed soaked in warm water. Also a quarter of a teaspoonful of cod-liver oil may be given with this meal.

Noon or Lunch-Time Give approximately one tablespoon of finely chopped, cooked meat; chicken, beef or rabbit are best as hearts and livers can upset a puppy's digestive system.

Teatime Feed the same as breakfast. If a complete puppy food was fed, soaked, at breakfast it could now be given dry for this meal.

Dinner Time This can be as lunch or a small amount of your own meal may be set aside specially for the puppy.

As the puppy grows and his appetite increases, so must his meals. But this must be done gradually, as a sudden increase may lead to a tummy upset. When using ready-prepared puppy foods, carefully follow the feeding instructions which the suppliers recommend, as both overfeeding and underfeeding can cause problems.

Six to Twelve Months Old

Once the puppy reaches six months of age it can be limited to three meals a day. Usually its teatime or third meal is omitted but the quantity of food at its three meals should be increased so that its overall intake remains the same.

When your puppy reaches twelve months old it should be reduced to two meals a day, but again care should be taken to see that the overall amounts remain the same.

Feeding the Adult Yorkie

Show dog or pet, the feeding requirements are very much the same. The most convenient way of feeding is to set aside a small bowl of food from your own meal, although this could present a bit of a problem if you own many dogs.

Today you can readily find a whole range of complete pre-prepared dog foods at the local pet shop. These products will require little or no preparation and so are convenient to use. Many people cook various kinds of meat for their dogs whether they have just a few or many to cater for. Putting meat into a large pan or a pressure cooker can be time-consuming and also requires much cleaning up afterwards but can be more economical when catering for a number of dogs. Should you decide to cook for your dog, you should be sure to add vitamins to his food to ensure he is getting enough of the correct nourishment.

Another alternative is a complete dry dog food which will suit your own dog. This will contain all the nourishment essential for your dog's health, including proteins, vitamins, calcium and other minerals, so you can be sure that he is getting a balanced meal. A protein level of around 16 per cent is required for an adult dog and a level of about 28 per cent for a growing puppy. Some breeders will feed their dogs and puppies on a complete dry dog food for every meal. Although this is perfectly acceptable, it may be a little boring for your dog. As dogs are carnivorous, some meat could be added to their diet. I prefer white meats for my own dogs although of course red meat can be given. This mixed diet of meat and prepared dry foods suits all my dogs' requirements. If you are not giving your dog a complete food you should add some form of vitamins to the food. Special dog vitamins are widely available from pet shops and can be purchased as tablets or powders making them easy to use. A vitamin supplement containing vitamin B is particularly good for stimulating a dog's appetite and so are useful when you have a poor eater. However, it is extremely important to adhere to the recommended dosage when adding vitamins as an overdose can be as harmful as a deficiency.

When purchasing ready-prepared dry dog foods be sure to select one that meets the needs of your dog. These foods normally range from 'puppy' to 'adult' with special mixtures available for a brood-bitch and even one for the overweight dog, this latter feed containing lower levels of protein and fat.

Food Facts

Whatever type of feeding you choose for your dog it is important to ensure that he receives a good balance of nutrients. In order to do this it is necessary to understand what is contained in the various foods you are giving him so you can ensure he is not missing some vital nutritional element.

Food	Contents
Beef (lean)	Protein, some fat, B group vitamins and some minerals.
Chicken	Protein, fat, vitamins and some minerals.
Tripe	Protein and fat.
Liver	Protein, fat, soluble fat, vitamins. Liver is not to be fed in excess.
Egg yolk	Most required nutrients.
Complete dry dog foods	Cereals, animal and vegetable proteins, concentrates, fats, vitamins and minerals.
Cereals	Carbohydrates (energy), proteins, a few vitamins and minerals.
Bones	Calcium, phosphorus, magnesium and protein.

Note: Bones should not be fed in excess as they can cause constipation and other intestinal problems. One bone a week, preferably a large marrowbone and not small bones that can splinter, such as chicken or fish bones, can be given.

Green Vegetables	Vitamin K
Cod-liver oil	Vitamins A, D and E.
Seaweed	Iodine which prevents hair loss and drowsiness.
Bone-meal	Calcium, phosphorus.

Vitamins

Vitamins are essential in a dog's diet, to promote good health and body functions. As dogs are unable to synthesize their own vitamins, it is important to be sure that they receive each through their diet on a regular basis. Carefully follow the instructions on the box or packet in determining the correct amounts and frequency of dose for your dog. Use the specially prepared dog vitamins and not the multi-vitamins widely available for adults. This is because the mixture of vitamins a dog needs is different from those required by humans. All vitamin supplements should be given in moderation, as an excess of some vitamins can be toxic and this may be very serious for a dog. A deficiency can also be very serious and can lead to various conditions.

Deficiency	Possible Consequences
Vitamin A	Night blindness and skin lesions.
Vitamin B	Anorexia, anaemia, weight loss, poor growth and convulsions.
Vitamin D	Rickets, osteomalacia and milk fever in nursing bitches.
Vitamin E	Infertility, anaemia and muscle weakness.

Proteins

Proteins are an important aspect of a dog's diet just as they are in a human's diet, providing as they do the building blocks for the body. Proteins are essential constituents of the cells which make up the body tissues and so play an important role in the development of muscle fibre. Proteins are essential for good growth in the coat and they help to keep the dog strong and aid the body's defence against disease. However, too much protein is unhealthy for a dog as it will make him fat and can cause other abnormalities as well, so it is important to use the correct amount of protein when feeding your dog.

An adult dog requires about 10 per cent of high-quality protein in his diet or about 12 to 14 per cent protein if choosing a complete dog food. Extra protein is required for pregnant and nursing bitches to give them strength and assistance in producing milk for their offspring. A puppy will require higher levels of proteins than an average adult in order to promote growth during its first few months of life. A diet consisting of between 24 and 33 per cent of protein is recommended for a growing puppy.

Minerals

A number of minerals are required by dogs in their diet, though they are only required in very small quantities. Various minerals can be found in a variety of common foods such as meats, cereals, green vegetables, fish, dairy produce and bones.

Fats

Fats also form an essential part of a dog's diet and the absence of fats in the diet can lead to all kinds of problems, from skin disorders to reproductive problems. Fat also enhances the palatableness of many foods and is used by fat-soluble vitamins such as vitamins A, B, E and K. Fats are a source of the essential fatty acids, which are required by the cells in the walls of the body. Fat in reasonable quantities is well digested by all healthy dogs, though fat in excess will destroy certain nutrients in a dog's diet and will lead to the dog putting on too much weight, which is unhealthy.

Carbohydrates

Research into the need for carbohydrates in a dog's diet is at the moment inconclusive. What is known is that while dogs are very good at burning up carbohydrates as an energy source they are not necessarily essential in a dog's diet. This is because dogs are able to synthesize their own glucose requirements from dietary fats and proteins, provided of course that these are present in sufficient quantities in the dog's diet. However, some research has claimed a need for a dietary source of carbohydrates in the case of pregnant bitches; the research claims that carbohydrates aid the bitch in producing a healthy litter.

Grooming

Grooming your Puppy

The practice of grooming the Yorkshire Terrier puppy begins at the tender age of eight to ten weeks and should be repeated twice a week at this stage. Regular grooming will enable the puppy to get used to being handled and so will aid training at a later date. Initially you will require just a dog comb for the grooming, a chrome comb with both coarse and fine teeth is ideal and readily available at all pet shops. With a puppy it is necessary to pay special attention to its chest, legs and its underside as it is these areas where the hair tends to tangle in dogs of this age.

While combing the puppy, lay it on its back on your lap so that it is facing you. Puppies are not particularly fond of this position and so may need some gentle persuasion at first. You will find this a good time to check the puppy's nails and the pads of its feet. With your puppy lying on its back you can now search for and see any tangles or mats on the underside. Having found a mat in the coat, begin to remove it by using your fingertips and gently teasing until it starts to break down. Once you have broken into the mat with your fingertips, use your comb to gently comb away the remaining pieces. Continue this process until all the mats have been removed.

When your puppy is clear of mats, stand it on a table keeping a firm hand on it always as a fall would severely injure such a young dog. With your puppy standing or sitting on the table, turn it so it is facing you and begin gently to comb him. You should comb the face, chin, throat and under the eyes while it is in this position. Remember to keep a hold on your puppy and do not, in any circumstances, walk away and leave it unattended because it may decide to follow you, especially since it is probably nervous about being groomed, so do take care.

Having finished combing the front of the puppy you should now turn it around 180 degrees so that it now has its back to you. With one hand, support your dog from the underneath and use your other hand gently to comb the sides and back. First you should use the coarse teeth on the comb then the finer section to finish off, always combing in a downwards direction. When one side is finished, swap hands and comb the other side using the same procedure. While you have your puppy standing on the table in front of you it is a good time to check that the anus is clean and free of any dry matter that may have accumulated. It is very important that this is checked regularly and cleared away as any slight blockage could get worse and forces the puppy to strain when trying to empty his bowels, so causing discomfort and possible internal injury. It also increases the risk of infection as it becomes easier for germs to find their way into the anus. Any dry matter found around the anus must therefore be removed by bathing or gently combing out; in extreme cases of hardened excreta it may be necessary to sit the dog in a bowl of warm water.

As a puppy's coat grows, more time and effort will be required in its grooming. Besides its hair getting longer, the puppy will become more active and hence more likely to tangle and matt its coat. Because of this, it is necessary to increase the frequency of the grooming sessions to three times a week or even to every day if required; the earlier a mat or tangle is tackled the easier it will be to remove. With the longer and thicker coat of the older puppy it may be necessary to give the dog's coat a good brushing with a firm bristle brush prior to combing in the regular way.

Bathing

Bathing a puppy can be a most enjoyable and a not too difficult experience. Just remember not to let the puppy lick the shampoo as this could give him an upset stomach, and subsequently diarrhoea, and also take care not to get shampoo in the puppy's eyes as this can sting and cause stress.

Place the puppy on the draining board, sink, or shower base and using lukewarm water soak the puppy's coat gently. Then, with a small amount of shampoo in one hand, and holding the puppy with the other, work the shampoo over the puppy's body, using the tips of your fingers to massage it into the skin. The shampoo should then be rinsed off with warm water and the whole process of shampooing and rinsing should be repeated. At this stage the coat should be conditioned, using a small amount of conditioner. This must then be rinsed off very carefully as any shampoo or conditioner left on the puppy's coat will not only make the coat look greasy and possibly scruffy, but will also irritate the skin.

Next, the puppy should be dried. Start by towel-drying him and then, with the use of a hair-drier and brush, gently dry his coat until it is completely dry. Remember this is a new experience for a puppy so hold it very firmly, but be very patient and do not be too rough. You will find that if the puppy is bathed regularly it will soon accept being bathed, although it may not like it. As the dog gets older and its coat grows, bathing will take longer and an adult dog with a long coat particularly needs a good-quality shampoo.

The length of the adult dog's coat makes drying a much more involved task and it is best to carry out any trimming of the moustaches while the hair is still wet and before drying begins. To dry the dog it is best to sit at a table with the dog on a towel placed on

Maureen and Dave Baldwin's Ch. Sharwin's Easter Dream.

your lap, his tail towards your body and the hair-drier placed on the table blowing towards the dog. Make sure that the drier does not blow on the same part of the dog's coat for too long as this may burn the skin and damage the coat. Brush the coat downwards and then part and repeat, moving downwards. Carry on this brushing and parting action all along the body until the coat is dry. The underside of the body and legs need similar attention. Stand the dog on your lap and allow the drier to blow on the chest and legs while brushing upwards and downwards on the legs. Make sure the whole body is dry, and remember that there must be no wrinkles or creases in the coat.

Grooming for the Show Ring

Grooming Equipment

There are a number of items you will need for everyday use in grooming your Yorkshire Terrier. These include:

A good-quality pair of scissors.
A comb with both wide and fine teeth.
Almond oil, a saucer and a pure-bristle brush, for oiling the coat while grooming and crackering.

Acid-free tissue paper cut into strips seven inches (17cm) long and two-and-a-half inches (7cm) wide.

Small elastic bands or fine pieces of string, to hold the tissue papers.

A pair of nail clippers, which can be either the guillotine type or the small pliers type.

A towel or a rubber mat, to stand the dog on while grooming.

Cotton wool, for wiping away tearstains from the eyes and cleaning the ears.

A baby's toothbrush and some doggy tooth-powder or paste.

Regular Grooming

Eyes Yorkshire Terriers need their eyes cleaned regularly – a small deposit of 'sleep' forming in the corner of the eyes is quite usual. If this is removed daily, no problem should arise. Sometimes when left in kennels for a couple of weeks or left with someone who does not realize that it should be removed, a large deposit can build up. This needs to be cleaned away with a little lukewarm water and cotton wool.

Ears The Yorkshire Terrier's ears should receive careful attention from a very tender age. The hair should be trimmed back from the point of the ear to approximately half-way down the flap. This promotes the correct ear carriage which is characteristic of the breed, and profuse hair on the ends of the puppy's ears can prevent them from assuming the correct position. The ears should be regularly cleaned with damp cotton wool and kept free from wax. Canker and mites, though not so prevalent in a prick-eared breed, can be kept at bay by the insertion of a few ear drops every four weeks. It is important to remember that when examining the ear in any way, one should not probe inside the ear as irreparable damage may be easily be done.

Nails and Pads Nails and pads should be checked every day. If your dog does not get much exercise on hard ground, his nails will soon grow long and can curl round into his pads. A pair of guillotine nail clippers are quite easy to use, although sometimes four hands are needed to hold the dog still. Dogs do get used to it and it does stop expensive vet's fees for a very simple procedure. However, to begin with, it would be wise to ask a more experienced person to show you how to clip a dog's nails because inexpert clipping can result in damage to the quick and cause bleeding. If in doubt, consult your vet.

Grass seeds and pine needles can pierce the dogs pads and set up an infection. These should be removed. Bathing daily in disinfectant diluted with warm water can help a lot but if the problem persists, it will have to be dealt with by your vet.

Grooming and Preparing the Show Coat

Although most Yorkshire Terriers will grow a moderately long coat, the coat must be cultivated in order to reach the much-desired length for the show ring. This means that time, patience and a lot of effort must be put into grooming. I personally think that the Yorkshire Terrier must be one of the hardest breeds to show, because apart from having to be blessed with the necessary virtues of the breed you need a dog who will tolerate being groomed, wearing paper crackers and one who will enjoy walking on a lead with his floor-length coat trailing. The length of this coat can sometimes cause problems: at all times between shows the adult Yorkshire Terrier will spend all of the time in crackers prior to grooming. Because of this you should re-member to exercise him occasionally when his coat is out of crackers between shows – this will teach him how to manage his coat when he is walking in the show ring.

The training and coat preparation for exhibition begins while the Yorkshire Terrier is just a few months old, and continues as he grows up until it becomes an everyday task. Some enjoy the fuss and atten-tion, while others just disappear when they see you preparing the grooming table. However, you should try to make it easy and enjoy-able for the dog and for yourself. Show grooming is a job that will require a fair amount of time and should never be done in a hurry. This especially applies to novices. Months of coat growing can be lost if the crackers are not put in correctly, or done up too tightly, or if the crackers on the face furnishings or topknot come off and he chews the hair, thus causing damage and breaking or shortening of the hair. Another danger to the coat is fleas as they will cause the dog to scratch and bite his coat. Time must always be allowed for checking these things.

Booties

The Yorkshire Terrier will need to wear what are known as boots or

Mrs Giddings' Ch. Mogid Millionairess.

booties to prevent him from scratching out the crackers. These are quite simple to make but should not be made out of anything but soft material because some materials, such as chamois leather, which dries stiff after getting wet, may cause discomfort to the dog's feet if he has trodden in a wet area. Take a piece of material from an old T-shirt or sock, cut this to about four inches (10cm) long and one and a half inches (4cm) wide, then fold it in half so that it looks like a finger cover. Sew down each side leaving the top open so you can put the dog's foot into it. One will be needed for each rear foot and should be fastened with a piece of surgical tape, but not so tightly as to stop the circulation from the leg to the foot. The booties should be changed daily as part of the grooming procedure, and immediately if the booties get wet.

Crackering the Yorkshire Terrier

This is very important in order to grow a good long coat for showing. Regular oiling of the coat must be carried out from a tender age. A little fine-texture oil should be used daily in order to keep the hair ends supple and thus promote coat growth. Most regular oil-based dressings can be used provided that they are safe to use on hair and skin. Different varieties can suit different coats and some oils can burn the skin giving a scurfy appearance. The oil should be lightly applied to the hair and should not completely drench it. A build-up of oil on the skin and coat will not do the coat any good, so the Yorkshire Terrier should be bathed every two to three weeks or you may experience difficulty in grooming. Failure to bath him regularly may result in the coat shedding large amounts of hair on the brush, or clogging up hair on the comb which is a sure sign that the dog is due for a bath.

At around five or six months, if the puppy has a sufficient amount of hair on the top of his head (the topknot), he can have a topknot cracker put in. Begin by combing all the hair on the top of the head in an upwards direction from the roots, taking a line from the corner of the eye back to the opening of the ear on both sides of the face, then a straight line at the back of the head from ear to ear; this almost creates a pyramid effect. Comb all the hair into the palm of your hand then wrap the hair in a strip of tissue paper, fold this up and put a band on it to hold it in place. Great care must be taken to ensure that the dog's hair is only held in place and not pulled too tightly, as any pressure may be painful to the puppy and will cause the puppy to scratch and rub his head. It may take a few days for him to accept wearing his topknot during which time, it may have to be replaced over and over again. Also at this stage booties can be put on to help prevent damage to the puppy's coat while breaking him in to the idea of wearing crackers.

Once the puppy has accepted the topknot, put a very small cracker in on either side of his mouth (moustache). Be sure that these crackers are put in so that they hang down; if they stick out or upwards, they are likely to go into the puppy's eyes when he is playing and running around. Also check that the hair is taken only from above the mouth, only going as far as the corner of the mouth, in line with the inside corner of the eye. Do not include the hair on the sides of the face. Be careful not to take any hair from under the chin as this can prevent the puppy from eating and drinking properly. Put a separate cracker under the chin (the beard). Take the chin-cracker hair from just under the chin, in line with the corners of the mouth, and fold the cracker. As the puppy grows, so should his hair and coat, and when he reaches between ten months and a year he can have crackers in the sides of his face (face furnishings) provided there is sufficient hair to hold a cracker. If there is not, it is better to wait until there is since premature crackering can do more damage than good.

At the time of putting in the face cracker there will be a need to start on the body. Put your dog on the grooming table and turn him away from you. Start with the tail (tail cracker) and be sure not to include any hair from the rump in this cracker; this cracker will help prevent the dog from getting a dirty bottom. Let the dog wear just this tail cracker for a few days before putting any more crackers on the body. Remember to comb it out and change the cracker each and every day otherwise the hair will mat up. Once the dog has accepted the tail cracker, crackers can be put in on either side of the rump (rump crackers). Start by taking a straight line down the loin as far as the stifle and then from the rump and from the top part of the back of the leg under the anus, put all this hair into one cracker, and be sure not to block the anus when putting in crackers for the rump and tail.

Next, move along the body about two inches (5cm) and comb a line down towards the table and put all this hair into another cracker (loin cracker). Moving forward along the body a further two inches, repeat the crackering procedure on the ribs (rib cracker). Then move on to the shoulder (shoulder cracker), the hair for the shoulder cracker should be taken from just above the shoulder, and just behind the shoulder and elbow. The next step is the neck (neck cracker) which is taken from behind the head and down to above the shoulder, this is

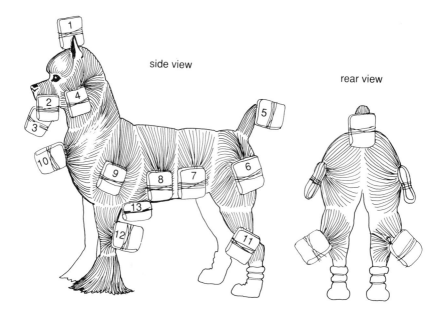

The crackered or wrapped Yorkie.

112

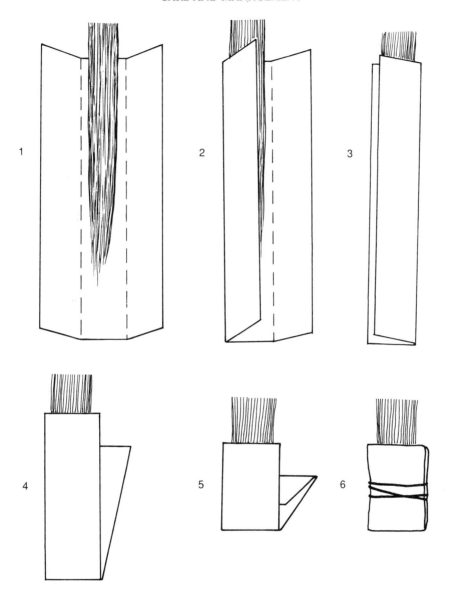

1

2

3

4

5

6

Preparing a Yorkie in paper. After folding a strip of paper into thirds and then reopening it: (1) rest hairs about half-way down the centre section; (2) fold one of the thirds over the centre section, not too tightly; (3) fold the other third over the centre section; then (4) fold the paper under once; (5) fold it under a second time; (6) put rubber bands around the final folded paper to keep it securely together. This is repeated as many as 20 times. In Britain this procedure is called crackering and in America is known as wrapping.

113

Ch. Ozmilion Dedication in crackers.

the only cracker that takes hair from both sides of the neck and is put just in the front of the dog under his head.

From here we go on to the legs, starting at the back with the stifle (stifle cracker). Gather all the tan hair, from the stifle to the hock, and put it into a cracker. Then move on to the elbow (elbow cracker) and take the hair from the elbow down to the pastern and place a cracker in here.

Follow this procedure on the other side of the dog. To finish off crackering you should lay the dog on his back and gather up the chest hair (chest cracker) and place the cracker.

This practice must be carried out on a daily basis if the coat is to be encouraged to grow: all the crackers must be taken out every day and the coat must be groomed and oiled (I always use almond oil) and finally crackered up again.

Use the diagram of the Yorkshire Terrier in crackers to help you find the position of the crackers and follow the names and numbers of the crackers.

Trimming the Show Coat

Trimming the adult Yorkshire Terrier's full coat is a job that should be done a week or two before a show and not the night before, unless

Mr J. Magri's Ch. BeeBee Mi Blase.

you are particularly skilled at trimming. The Yorkshire Terrier's coat will probably be longer on one side than the other; this, I believe, is because the side on which the dog sleeps tends to be shorter. However, if the coat is very long and covering the floor, it may prevent your dog moving well in the show ring and especially on grass which can cause a big problem if the coat is extraordinarily long. The procedure for trimming the coat is best practised after a bath. Dry and prepare the dog just like you are going to show it – with a centre parting down his back, from the occiput to the root of the tail. Stand him on the edge of a high table with one side of his coat hanging over the side. This job requires two people, one to stand the dog as if showing on his box at a show, and the other person to trim the coat with a sharp pair of quality scissors.

Having first combed the coat out, start at the front end on one side and cut along the coat towards the rear. You should make these cuts just where it hangs over the side of the table so that his new trim is just to the ground. Turn the dog around and repeat this procedure on his other side. Next you should pay attention to the rear end of the dog. Turn him so that he is facing away from you and comb the hair from the tail and rear end, so that it hangs over the side of the table. You should now cut across in a straight line but be sure to start with a curve and end with a curve. Once you have trimmed the body all the way around, you should attend to the face furnishings and moustache. Start by having the dog facing you and comb all the hair so it hangs off the edge of the table, and then cut straight across but again starting with a curve and ending in a curve.

When this has been completed comb the coat out all over and tidy up any scraggy ends that might have been missed. Then oil and cracker the main body coat leaving the chest hair and the hair on the legs. Comb the chest hair down on to the table and trim to ground level.

Next you should trim the leg hair. Starting with the front legs, comb the hair from the elbow down to the table then trim just slightly above the table top. You should repeat this procedure on the hind legs with the hair from the stifle being cut to the same table-top length. Then cracker up the hair on all four legs. Finally just trim around the feet; make these cuts as if you are cutting around a coin and try to avoid giving a rabbit foot like appearance to the feet as this is undesirable.

5

Showing

Why Show?

Show people are often asked why they get so involved in the world of showing dogs, with its theatrical and often circus-like atmosphere. For many the simple answer is the fame and glamour. A very dear old friend of mine, Bill Sigger, once said to me that in his opinion many people with failed aspirations to the stage and screen ended up in the show ring; I feel that there is much truth in this. It is also true that the vast majority of people show out of love for their dogs and a genuine desire to improve the breed, as dog showing is a time-consuming and expensive hobby.

Whatever motivation leads you to your first show, it is assured that the excitement of competition will take hold, the bug will bite, and each successive show will be as tense and thrilling as the first. It is at a dog show where a comparison can be made between the immaculate model of presentation, assuming a regal stance on a red velvet box, and the lively, merry and often untidy pet. This glossy image of perfection has attracted many a new recruit to the absorbing interest of dog showing and the dedicated pursuit of preparing the Yorkshire Terrier for exhibition.

For a breeder, a visit to a Championship show gives him a chance to compare the quality of his own exhibits with those of other, more experienced breeders and to show fellow exhibitors the best of his home-bred stock. His well-presented, high-quality exhibits are the best advertisement for his kennel, enabling him to find stud-work for his dogs. The exciting experience of winning a red card is, of course, the ultimate delight for any fancier, a pleasure that can be shared equally by the seasoned exhibitor and novice alike. Many exhibitors, however, travel the show circuit over the length and breadth of the country frequently, without even receiving any of the major awards. It is this dedication to a chosen breed and the maintenance of its standards that must be responsible for the excellence of dog breeding.

On the lighter side, showing can be a lot of fun as a hobby which can be enjoyed by the whole family or just an individual. Yorkshire Terriers are a very good breed for competition. If you are about to embark on a show career for the first time, I suggest you go along to a couple of events to get an idea of what it entails before you make your first entry. If you can accompany an experienced owner who is showing, so much the better. It is also a good idea to join a club which specializes in the breed (*see* Appendix 2, page 231).

The care and preparation of a show dog obviously requires special attention above that required for the average pet companion. The various aspects of the dog show and the special treatment your dogs will need are discussed in this chapter. These include: training, types of shows and classes, preparations and, finally, your big day at the show.

To qualify for entry into shows your dog must be six months old at least and registered in your name at the Kennel Club.

Types of Show

Having made the decision to show your dog, you will have to find a suitable show in which to enter him as there are various types of shows that take place. In Great Britain all shows are run under Kennel Club rules; in other countries, shows are controlled by the respective countries' own ruling body. A list of these can be found in Appendix 2 at the back of this book (*see* page 231–3). The types of show that are currently held in Great Britain are as follows:

Exemption Shows

These are run with the permission of the Kennel Club but do not strictly adhere to the Kennel club rules. They are most often held in conjunction with small agricultural shows, fêtes or small fund-raising activities. They offer a few classes for pedigree dogs and most often a variety of novelty classes in which non-pedigree dogs are allowed to compete. They provide excellent training for novice exhibitors and likewise their dogs.

Sanction Shows

These can have up to twenty-five classes if for more than one breed,

Pauline Osbourne's Ch. Polliam Sweet Delight.

or up to ten if for a single breed. The classification will be such that dogs who have won extensively at larger shows will be unable to compete, which gives the novice exhibitor a greater opportunity for success.

Limited Shows

As the name suggests, these shows are limited to members of the society or club responsible for organizing the show, or occasionally to people residing within certain areas. Dogs who have won Challenge Certificates are inelligible for competition in these shows.

Open Shows

Open shows vary in size enormously, but in every case the classification is open to all pedigree dogs. Many Open Shows attract a large entry of champion exhibits and the competition may be almost as keen as that of a Championship Show.

119

Championship Shows

Championship shows are the largest and most competitive of all dog shows. It is only at these shows that the Challenge Certificates which raise a dog to the status of champion are awarded and consequently only the cream of the canine world compete for these honours. They may be for a single breed or for numerous breeds.

Cruft's Cruft's is the largest and most famous of all the Championship Shows. Dog breeders and exhibitors from all over the world flock to this great show, year in and year out, to see the very best of the British dog world. Each year this show becomes evermore popular and receives greater attention and publicity through the television, radio and newspaper media. It was at one time rather difficult to qualify to enter Cruft's as the qualification criterion was a first prize in certain classes at a major Championship Show. So in order to qualify, the exhibitors would race around the country entering every show until they had won and so qualified for entry into Cruft's. Fortunately the qualification has now been relaxed and so it is no longer so difficult to enter this show.

The Various Classes

At any one show there will be many classes and each will have different entry criteria. These classes generally group the dogs by age, experience, sex or ownership. Definitions of the classes are given below and often have sections for both dog and bitch in each class.

Minor Puppy For dogs of six and not exceeding nine calendar months of age on the day of the show.

Puppy For dogs of six and not exceeding twelve calendar months of age on the day of the show.

Junior For dogs of six and not exceeding eighteen calendar months of age on the day of the show.

Maiden For dogs who have not won a Challenge Certificate or a first prize at an Open Championship Show (Puppy, Special Puppy, Minor Puppy and Special Minor Puppy classes excepted).

The author's favourite picture of Ch. Ozmilion Dedication winning Reserve Best in Show at the Scottish Kennel Club Championship Show under the famous all-rounder judge Albert Langley; presenting the trophy is Mrs Joyce Mann. Left: Mrs J. Tattersall with her most famous Ch. Olac Moon Pilot.

Novice   For dogs who have not won a Challenge Certificate or three or more first prizes at Open and Championship Shows (Minor Puppy, Special Minor Puppy, Puppy and Special Puppy classes excepted, whether restricted or not).

Undergraduate   For dogs who have not won a Challenge Certificate or three or more first prizes at Championship Shows (Puppy, Special Puppy, Minor Puppy and Special Minor Puppy classes excepted).

Graduate   For dogs who have not won a Challenge Certificate or four or more first prizes at Championship Shows in Graduate, Post-Graduate, Minor Limit, Mid-Limit, Limit and Open classes, whether restricted or not.

Mid-Limit   For dogs who have not won three Challenge Certificates or five or more first prizes in all Championship Shows in Mid-Limit, Limit and Open Classes confined to the breed, whether restricted or not, at shows where CCs were offered for the breed.

Limit For dogs who have not won three Challenge Certificates under three different judges or seven or more first prizes in all, at Championship Shows in Limit and Open Classes confined to the breed, whether restricted or not, at shows where Challenge Certificates were offered for the breed.

Open For all dogs of the breeds for which the class is provided and eligible for entry at the show.

There may also be some special classes at the show such as: Beginners, for exhibits not having won a First at the club's shows; Not Bred by Exhibitor; Brace, for a pair of dogs; Team, for two or more dogs; Veteran, for dogs of not less than seven years of age on the day of the show; Breeders, for dogs bred by the exhibitor.

Awards at Shows

At all shows there will be many awards made by the judges, within each class. The top five entries will be placed in order: First, Second, Third, Reserve (Fourth) and Very Highly Commended (Fifth). A prize card will be awarded to these top five entries and, at an Open, Limit or Club Show, a rosette may be presented to the first three positions.

A dog who wins a First in his class or classes automatically becomes eligible for what is called the Challenge. This Challenge would be for the Best of Breed in an Open or Limit Show and for Best in Show at a Club Show. In the Challenge the judge will choose both a First and a Reserve and these will receive a prize card and a rosette. At Championship Shows it is a little different: all first-prize winners (sometimes including the second-prize winner from the Open class) challenge for the Challenge Certificate (CC); a First and a Reserve will be awarded. This procedure will take place for both dog and bitch. The winners of each CC will then compete against each other for the Best of Breed award.

The next stage for the Best of Breed Yorkshire Terrier would be to compete against the other Best of Breed toy dogs in the show. The eventual winner of this Best in Group section will go on to meet the winners of all the other groups to determine the overall winner, the Best in Show; a Reserve Best in Show will also be awarded. Prize money is often awarded at shows but is usually a nominal amount, often less than the entry fee, so profit is not a reason to be competing in the show ring. Sometimes there may be trophies and gifts to be competed for, but most exhibitors are there for the prestige of winning and the great joy of showing their dogs.

Show Training

Your dog must be in tiptop condition before showing; if he is not fully prepared to the highest standard he should not be entered. He must be able to stand properly and he must be lead broken – no judge will pick a dog who will not stand properly or walk well no matter how wonderful he looks. The dog must tolerate close examination of his teeth and feet and general bone structure. Remember, a show dog

Author with the youngest champion in the breed at 13½ months old, Ch. Ozmilion Premonition.

123

must be just that in every sense of the word; you must know every inch of your dog and be able to make an honest assessment of his faults and strong points.

It is important that your dog enjoys his early shows; early mistakes should not be considered as set-backs but as valuable lessons which are good for experience. Listen to criticism from well-meaning friends who will notice faults which you may not. The novice owner must be aware that he is also on show and that his performance as a handler will complement or detract from that of his dog. A little style and showmanship by both man and dog as a team will add to the occasion.

Having decided on a show career, it is your responsibility to ensure that your dog is properly trained and prepared to make the best of his potential in the ring. The show ring is not the place for training and he must have mastered the elements of ringcraft before his first entry. He must be trained to walk and stand properly both on the ground and on the table and he must be accustomed to being examined and handled by strangers. Ringcraft training is often available through local dog clubs. Only time and effort spent on these aspects when the puppy is young will provide the background to a sound future performance.

Table Training

Put the puppy on to the covered table or covered show box and keep a firm hand on him to give him confidence. At first he will probably just lie flat as he may feel insecure, so you must reassure him and make him realize that he is safe. Soon he will stand and look around him – take care at this stage that he does not fall off the table. Use commands such as 'Up' or 'Table', this will get him used to the lift and to expect the handling, grooming or examination that is to follow. Once the puppy is used to all this he can be taught to stand properly for examination.

Lead Training

At first the puppy will not accept the lead and will probably just lie flat and refuse to move. If this happens give him lots of encouragement, getting down to his level if needed. Be patient, as time spent now will be well rewarded later. Eventually, he will need to be taught to walk on your left for showing. You must get the puppy used to

18 CLASS UNBENCHED OPEN SHOW SUNDAY 20TH JANUARY Held under Kennel Club Rules & Show Regulations	ON NO ACCOUNT WILL ENTRIES BE ACCEPTED WITHOUT FEES	PLEASE USE SEPARATE FORM FOR EACH OWNER	ENTRY FEES: MEMBERS £1.75 Per Dog 1st class 50p subsequent classes same dog NON-MEMBERS £2.25 Per Dog 1st class 60p subsequent classes same dog ENTRIES CLOSE: MONDAY 17TH DECEMBER (1st Class Post)

INSTRUCTIONS: This form must be used by one person only (or partnership) Writing MUST BE IN INK OR INDELIBLE PENCIL. Use one line only for each dog. The name of the dog and all the details as recorded with the Kennel Club must be given on this entry form. If an error is made the dog may be disqualified by the Committee of the Kennel Club. All dogs must be REGISTERED at the Kennel Club and if a Registered dog has changed ownership the TRANSFER must be registered before the date of the show. A Puppy under 6 months old cannot be exhibited. When entering more than one breed or variety use, if possible, a separate form for each. On no account will entries be accepted without fees.

REGISTERED NAME OF DOG	BREED	SEX D. or B.	FULL DATE OF BIRTH	BREEDER	SIRE (BLOCK LETTERS)	DAM (BLOCK LETTERS)	TO BE ENTERED IN CLASSES NOS.

For Exhibitor's use:	ONE LINE FOR EACH DOG. PUT CLASSES IN NUMERICAL ORDER. CHECK ALL DETAILS BEFORE POSTING.	BLOCK LETTERS
Entries @ £1.75	DECLARATION	Name of Owner(s) _____
Entries @ 50p	I/We undertake to abide by the Rules and Regulations of the Kennel Club and of this show and not to bring to the show any dog which has contracted or been knowingly exposed to any infectious or contagious disease during the six weeks prior to the day of the show. Any dog which I/we exhibit will only be prepared for exhibition in accordance with the requirements of Kennel Club Regulations for the Preparation of Dogs for Exhibition F (B).	Address _____
Entries @ £2.25		
Entries @ 60p		
Membership		
New Members		Telephone _____
Advertisement _	Usual Signature of Owner(s)	
TOTAL £	Date	
CHEQUE/P.O./CASH	NOTE: Dogs entered in breach of Kennel Club Show Regulations are liable to disqualification whether or not the Owner was aware of the breach. FEES PAYABLE TO:	

Show entry form.

125

walking on any surface whether hard or soft, as shows are held both indoors and out, often on grass which is not really suitable for Yorkshire Terriers as they will collect grass cuttings and leaves in their long flowing coats. However, you must prepare your dog for every eventuality so it is a good idea to walk him on cut and longish grass during training.

Entering Shows

Shows are normally advertised in weekly publications such as *Dog World* and *Our Dogs*. The type of show will be indicated in the advertisements and these will also include the show secretaries' names, addresses and telephone numbers. It is the secretaries who will provide schedules and entry forms. Along with the entry form you will receive a list of the classes at the show and the rules and regulations that govern entry to the various classes and to the show in general. The cost of entry to the various classes will be stated as will instructions for filling out the entry form. Typically, the entry form will ask you for various details including:

Name and address
Registration name and dog
Breed of dog
Sex: dog or bitch
Date of birth of your dog
Breeder
Sire and Dam of your dog
Which classes you wish to enter for.

You will also be asked to sign a declaration stating that you agree to abide by the rules and regulations of the show. Once the entry form is complete you must forward it with your entry fee to the secretary before the closing date, which is normally one month before the show for an Open or Limit show and two months in the case of a Championship Show.

Preparing for the Show

The novice's first show is bound to be a nerve-racking experience, but remember that even the most successful and experienced owners had to start out in this position, and were undoubtedly just as nervous. Every attempt must be made not to allow your nervous state to be transmitted down the lead to your dog as this will only worsen his own state and make the start to his show career a less than happy experience.

A lot can be learnt at this early stage by careful observation of the more experienced handlers at work in the ring, but it is important for you to be critical and not to pick up their bad points. Many handlers allow their dogs to develop and maintain bad habits and idio-syncracies which can detract from their performance in the ring. The novice owner must learn to recognize the faults in other dogs and not allow them in his own. Any which are spotted should be discouraged at the earliest stage, with care being taken not to stifle the extrovert nature which you are trying to encourage.

A lot of the anxiety associated with your first showing can be eliminated by careful planning beforehand. This coupled with actively seeking advice from other show people will go a long way to ensure a relatively painless début. As journeys are inevitably in-volved in entering shows it is important to accustom your dog to travelling; if he suffers from travel sickness do not feed him before the journey.

As an owner about to enter your first show you are probably asking yourself what, apart from the dog, should you take. Obviously several things will spring to mind immediately and subsequent expe-rience will dictate your final list. In the meantime here are some suggestions, starting with the show box itself. This should be about $18 \times 12 \times 12$ inches ($45 \times 30 \times 30$cm) and enclosed on all sides except the front which should have a wire-mesh door with a secure fasten-ing. The show box serves as a transit case and as a box on which the dog is presented; it may even double as a kennel at home. A fabric cover must be made for the box and this may have pockets provided for a brush and comb. The cover is traditionally red in colour, but this is not the rule. Your dog will be used to his box and it will provide him with security in a strange environment.

You will need to take towels and a blanket or rug for the dog to sleep on along with the food and water bowls and of course, his food and water for the day. Among the smallest but equally important items you will need are pure bristle brushes, a metal comb and acid-free tissue paper for wrapping the dog's coat. Various elastic bands including the orthodontic variety for the topknot, and a mist water spray. You will also require ribbon for the dog's topknot; this should,

Joyce Mann's Ch. Craigsbank Miss Dior.

of course, match the box cover. A fine, silk show lead of the slip-on variety will be needed for the ring as will a clip or pin with which to fasten your ring number.

Remember to check that you have all of your equipment before leaving and do not neglect your own needs. A flask containing hot soup or drink and some food plus extra warm clothing will prove invaluable during the long periods of waiting at the show. Finally plan your journey time, allowing extra time and never, never arrive late on the day of the show.

At the Show

On arrival at the venue there is much to do prior to entering the ring and a routine must be established; this will come with experience. We all have our own way of doing things but I will outline some of the important steps which must be followed.

Firstly you will need to find out where the toy dogs are to be benched and find out your position and bench number from the entry

Veronica Sameja-Hilliard's Ch. Verolian Al Pacino.

pass or the catalogue. Now is a good time to take your dog out of his box for some exercise and a chance to relieve himself, let him have a good look around and show him the ring. This will give him a chance to settle into this strange environment; remember that the novice dog may find the whole experience a little overwhelming. Do not forget to check the show catalogue to ensure your entry has been correctly listed and that the entry is free from printer's errors. Any errors found must be brought to the notice of the show secretary immediately.

Now is a good time to lay out your equipment and start the grooming process. Remove the wrappings from the dog's coat and damp the coat to remove any wrinkles, giving the coat a good brushing to bring up the gloss and then allowing the dog to rest. Leave the final preparations, such as the topknot and final grooming until one or two classes before entering the ring. When you are sure you have prepared your dog to the best advantage take him and your box, cover and grooming equipment to the ringside. The steward will give you your ring number and from then on you must only concern yourself with your exhibit and the judge.

Procedure in the Ring

On entering the ring join the line of waiting competitors and present your dog on his box and then wait for the judge to call you to the table. Remember to take your brush for the judge to use. Here he will closely examine the dog and once satisfied, will ask you to walk him. Listen very carefully to the judge's instructions and return with the dog to your box when he has finished with you.

It is important to know what the judge will look for when you are showing your dog. He will initially look for a dog who most closely resembles the Breed Standard. He will also look at the general performance of the dog, at the way he walks, stands and presents himself; his alertness and temperment, and the overall presentation.

With experience it becomes second nature for a judge to assess the relative merits of the dogs being shown. Obviously some factors of a dog's appearance are more important than others, the following is a guide to the relative importance of the different physical qualities of a dog when being judged in the show arena.

Value of Points in Judging

Formation and terrier appearance	15
Colour of hair on body	15
Richness of tan on head and legs	15
Quality and texture of coat	10
Quality of length of coat	10
Head	10
Mouth	5
Legs and feet	5
Ears	5
Eyes	5
Tail (carriage of)	5
	100

What Makes a Good Dog Great?

1. The handler in the show ring – go to shows and study exactly how they get the best out of their dogs.
2. The maintenance and care of the dog at home from his earliest days.

3. A sense, which is only developed by practice, of being able to visualize exactly what the judge sees when he looks at your exhibit. It rgoes without saying that you should only show the very best of your dogs.

4. Do not show your dog until he is ready to be seen. It is no good saying he will be all right later, he should definitely be in with a very good chance of winning on that day. If not, he should stay at home until he is really ready to come out winning. Of course it does not always work but it is hopeless going to a show with a lot of doubts.

5. Give yourself plenty of time when you arrive, so that you and the dog can relax.

6. Do not get him ready too soon and make him stand around for hours – he will only get bored.

7. Remember, Yorkshire Terriers are very intelligent, so you must make it fun for your show dog. This way he will really enjoy showing himself off, not just stand there wondering to himself how long it is going to go on.

8. Do not spoil your show dog by using him at stud. Very few dogs can do both jobs. Over use of your stud-dog will impair your dog's performance and condition for the show ring. He will become much more interested in the opposite sex and will not co-operate.

Judging

After some years of showing good dogs, exhibitors are sometimes asked to consider judging a few classes of their breed at a small show. If all goes well, they will usually be asked to judge again and all these judging appointments should be carefully recorded in a book, giving all the details of the number of dogs and entries for future reference.

Initially all judges should start their careers as breed specialists having been breeders themselves, eventually becoming all-round judges as their career and experience grows.

When you are judging you will be provided with a judging book which will have the number of dogs entered in each class list. Judging takes place in the order of this schedule.

The judge's word is final. He must not make any public commentary while judging, although he may talk to exhibitors after the show as some people like to ask the judge's opinion on their own dogs. Also the judge is required to write a report of his decisions (a critique) which will then be published in the national dog press.

The author's Ch. Ozmilion My Infatuation.

As a judge, you are judging the dogs on that particular day and that is what you must do. It does not matter what they have won before; it is their performance on the day that you must judge. Take your time and give each exhibit a thorough examination, even if it has very little hope of winning. All the exhibitors have paid the same money for your opinion and they each deserve equal treatment. Be firm but gentle and give all the exhibitors time for a final groom before the last assessment and making your placements.

When judging do not fault-judge (assess dogs according to their faults rather than their virtues). By fault-judging you could easily end up with something mediocre as your winner. Rather, look at the whole dog, note his good points while bearing in mind his failings, and compare him with the rest of the entries. This way you will select a good, worthy winner with many fine qualities.

You may have to give first prize to a dog you do not particularly like, but who is the best in his class. If the dogs are really bad then, unpopular as it might be, the prize card should be withheld. Remember, every time you judge, you are being judged. If people like your judging, gradually you will be asked to judge more and more regularly, until one day you actually award CCs in your bread. This is an

Mr Joe Magri with his Ch. Emotions of Rozamie at Ozmilion.

honour and should never be taken lightly; the future of the breed is partly in your hands. Your winners, by virtue of their wins under your judging that day, could figure in someone's breeding programme.

Every judge has to sign the Kennel Club Challenge Certificate and Reserve Certificate to say that in his opinion, the recipient is worthy to hold the title of Champion. If he is not, then the certificate should not be awarded. Yorkshire Terriers are popular in many countries and if your judging is liked you may be asked to officiate in other countries. The respective Kennel Clubs write to each other to check your details and if all is in order, the invitation is confirmed. This can be a most exciting and satisfying experience.

6

Breeding

First-Time Breeders

Before deciding to breed, much thought must be given to all the different aspects of breeding so that you can work towards this goal of producing the perfect Yorkshire Terrier. It is important that you examine your reasons for breeding before embarking on a breeding programme. Breeding can be an expensive, time-consuming hobby, not to be undertaken lightly.

Great care must be taken in the selection of the brood-bitch and also the stud-dog that will mate with her. The time for the mating and the actual mating itself will have to be planned. Once pregnant, the expectant dam will have certain needs that you will have to cater for. When the due day arrives you must be prepared for the whelping and be aware of what may go wrong and what action to take if it does. Once the whelping is complete your responsibilities are still far from over: you must see that both mother and puppies are healthy and developing well and you must also be prepared to wean the puppies. Once the puppies have been weaned you then have the responsibility of creating or finding good homes for them.

Having decided to breed, the aim should be to breed good, healthy examples of the Yorkshire Terrier who represent the Breed Standard as closely as possible, while attempting to make every litter an improvement on the last. In order to work towards the high standards already existing in the breed, new breeders should seek as much help and assistance as they can. To begin breeding with no previous experience or guidance can be an expensive and disappointing lesson. In order to avoid or minimize the disappointment, the new breeder should seek advice from experienced breeders and take time to learn and understand the Yorkshire Terrier Breed Standard, which is their goal.

Background to Breeding

It should be remembered that the Yorkshire Terrier is a man-made breed which only dates back to the latter part of the nineteenth century. The current breed's ancestry certainly lies with larger dogs, an example being the famous Huddersfield Ben who was recorded in 1883 at 12 pounds (5.5kg) in weight, considerably heavier than to-day's Standard.

It would also appear that earlier breeders looked to colour and texture of coat as main attributes in championship-winning dogs. Unfortunately this obsession with the coat led to a neglect of the other physical characteristics when selecting breeding partners, and this led to many dogs exhibiting less than straight toplines, with bodies ill-proportioned to their legs, and poor movement and spirit.

Another and a more serious result of this preoccupation with the coat was that the breed's heredity problems were often overlooked and even multiplied by careless breeders. It is clear that if breeders concentrate on one single characteristic of a dog to the exclusion of basic soundness, movement, spirit and type, they are surely walking the rocky road to ruin.

The novice breeder should be wary of perpetuating or, worse, exacerbating the problems associated with heredity. These problems include physical defects such as patella luxation (slipping kneecap, slipping stifle) which is possibly recessively inherent in the breed. This can often be indicated by the intermittent lifting of one or both of the hind legs during running or walking. It would, of course, be sensible not to breed from animals afflicted with this condition.

Other possibly inherent faults to consider when selecting breeding partners concern the dog's characteristics and personality traits. A good show dog needs a bright and endearing personality coupled with the ability to tolerate handling by strange judges and the proximity of other dogs. It would obviously be foolhardy to breed a dog and bitch who both display or have a history in their lines of the same character defect or personality trait such as excessive timidity or aggression, persistent barking and the like.

Most, if not all, inherent faults can be eradicated through careful selection and the employment of good breeding systems. There are three options or systems open to breeders and these are known as in-breeding, line-breeding and outcrossing. Every breeder must have a clear understanding of what each system means and the advantages, disadvantages and main purpose of each one.

Susan Prevost with her Hassandean Youngsters.

In-breeding

In-breeding is the mating of very closely related dogs, for instance, father to daughter, mother to son or brother to sister. This system should only be practised by the most experienced breeder and then only if he is totally sure of the faults and qualities which lie behind several generations of the stock to be used. In-breeding will very quickly stamp the best qualities of the parents on the succeeding generations, but it will just as quickly reproduce the faults, and may even exacerbate them.

It would be unwise for any breeder to attempt this system without several years of experience behind him, and then only to reproduce definite characteristics. In-breeding carries far too great an element of risk to be attempted without a great deal of knowledge.

Line-breeding

Line-breeding is the most widely accepted system of producing quality stock. It is the mating of dogs with one or more common relatives in their pedigree, with the view to instilling the virtues carried in their background with an ever-increasing permanence in the future generations.

This is a less risky system than direct in-breeding and less haphazard than the complete outcross. Results from line-breeding may not be as good as those from skilful in-breeding but they will be better than those from poor in-breeding.

Line-breeding is basically the system on which most of the top breeding kennels in any breed of pedigree dogs has been established, and this is probably the safest method for the average novice breeder to adopt. However, line-breeding reproduces the faults equally as strongly as the good points and this should be borne in mind carefully when selecting the two examples of any line which are to be mated.

If you feel that your bitch carries the blood-lines you would be happy to found your kennels on, select a dog which is of similar breeding and who is nearest to the standard of quality you have in mind. Do not be tempted to select a certain dog just because he is currently being shown in the ring; he may not be best at siring the highest-quality puppies. It is better to select a proven sire who is dominant in the qualities that are weak in your own stock. Always try to keep uppermost in your mind a balanced image of the type you are trying to achieve, and never forget the folly of obsession with one particular aspect of the breed to the detriment of the others.

Outcrossing

This is the mating of totally unrelated dogs. The outcross is sometimes used by breeders of toy dogs to restore strength, soundness or size to a line which the breeder feels has been closely bred for too many generations.

It is generally true that this system carries the greatest element of trial and error and the results can be somewhat unpredictable. Outcrossing cannot be recommended to the novice who wishes to produce stock for the show ring, and in general is not practised by the majority of breeders who achieve success in this field.

The Breeder's Responsibilities

Over the last thirty years there has been a huge population explosion in the breed and as I write this book in 1990, we must look forward to the future of the breed in the twenty-first century. I think that the following points will become increasingly important in the years to come:

1.   Breeders should not mate their bitch unless there is a good chance of a resultant improvement in the next generation.
2.   Breeders should not mate their bitch too often. Never turn her into a breeding machine.
3.   Stud-dog owners should never have a dog at stud with an hereditary fault approaching anything of a serious nature, such as vicious tendencies, or one with unsoundness such as slipping patellas or hip dysplasia. Only dogs with perfect mouths should be permitted to sire the next generation.
4.   Sell puppies only to genuine people. If you are in doubt, withdraw the puppy from sale. You may upset the intending purchaser but your responsibility to the puppy you have brought into the world is more important.
5.   Never breed from the second generation of a fault. If it has already passed through two generations, the genes must be very strong and it is up to you to make sure it will not be passed to a third generation.
6.   Do not keep more dogs than you can look after properly. You are not being fair to yourself or to the dogs.
7.   Stud-dog owners must never mate poor-quality bitches. There is a standard below which a bitch just does not have anything to offer the breed.
8.   Breed only from dogs and bitches that could be seen in the show ring. By this I do not necessarily mean that they could be top winners – they could be a bit on the large size for showing but apart from that, should be good representatives of the breed.

The Stud-Dog

On the whole the new breeder would be well advised to rely on the services of the established breeding kennels rather than to invest in the purchase of his own stud-dog. When he has acquired a considerable level of breeding experience then the decision can be made either to buy or to breed his own stud-dog. The correct choice is vital and only a dog displaying absolute excellence and championship quality stands a chance of becoming a worthwhile stud.

During the period of 'going out' prior to maintaining his own stud-dog the new breeder must take equal care in the selection of the potential stud-dog at the chosen kennel. If possible, a viewing of the dog's pedigree should be arranged. It would be useful if you have knowledge of the sire's progeny. The dog currently winning in the show ring should not necessarily be the automatic choice as the partner for your bitch. The dog's sire may prove to be a better choice, especially if it has sired other quality puppies. Having said this, the new breeder should always be on the look-out for that 'star quality' when selecting the stud-dog. All the best show dogs have that special sparkle and character that lifts them above their peers of equal breed quality. This extra asset which lifts them above the rest is generally evident at the puppy stage and appears as extrovert and lively behaviour and often a cheeky, endearing charm. It is important to recognize and develop these traits from an early stage.

Once the new breeder has acquired sufficient experience to consider owning his own stud-dog he will have to decide between choosing an experienced stud-dog with proven quality progeny or developing a younger dog of excellent quality and potential. The future stud will need plenty of love and freedom. He should be encouraged to play and to socialize with other dogs. Remember he is a dog and an extrovert male character should be positively encouraged and developed. It would be useful to enter him for some shows when he is ready as this will help to keep him friendly and good natured with other dogs and people under demanding conditions.

You will need to ensure that the dog gets plenty of daily exercise to maintain good muscle tone and condition linked to a well-balanced, high-protein diet. Remember that the aim is to develop a dog who will never refuse to mount a bitch who is presented in a ready condition. He will instinctively try to mount another dog and should never be reprimanded for this behavior in adolescence as this may lead to unwillingness to perform when you want him to.

The young dog's first real experience should be planned for ten months old or later. His first service should be an easy and enjoyable experience, and this can be aided by the use of an experienced bitch. It would be sensible to hold the bitch securely during the mating. The use of a young maiden at this stage could prove a difficult and frustrating time for owner and dog alike, not to mention the potential damage to the stud. It is easy to teach a young dog what is expected of him with the help of a co-operative bitch and some gentle handling.

A stud-dog's second experience should arrive several months later so as not to over-tax his virility. Reluctance or failure at his first opportunity should not be corrected by force or reprimand; patience and persistence is needed at this stage. Continue the attempts every couple of months or until he shows by his actions that he is ready. Once fully matured, a good stud-dog can be mated without stress at least once if not twice a week if he is very virile. It is not, however, advisable to allow too much activity from a dog who is being shown as he may lose weight and coat. A healthy stud can mate successfully for many years but his sperm will begin to lessen in fertility after about ten years, depending on the condition of the dog and how he is kept.

The Brood-Bitch

The idea of getting a brood-bitch is that she will be the foundation of your stock or blood-line. This is very important to remember, as any serious faults that are carried by this bitch are going to be passed on to future generations and this can be both very disheartening and very discouraging, especially for the beginner. As a prospective breeder you would be best advised to be patient and study form and pedigrees while attending some dog shows, preferably Championship Shows, where you can see some of the breed's best exhibits. You must also study the Yorkshire Terriers in general to see which lines and type appeal to your taste, speak to the breeders and obtain as much information on the breed as possible. Do not be too hasty and eager to spend your money as this is a very important move for your future as a breeder. Once you have taken the time and have given much thought to your brood-bitch you should purchase the best you can afford.

The brood-bitch, apart from being healthy, and clear from any skin problems, should have a good sound temperament and a kind and loving disposition. She must have sound hindquarters and her pelvic bone (pelvis) should be wide enough to pass a puppy. She should have a good mouth, and a good solid body and she should not be too narrow in the back. She should be as close in appearance to the Standard as possible, preferably weighing somewhere between 5 and 7 pounds (2 and 3kg). It is not advisable to breed from tiny bitches under 5 pounds, as this may cause unnecessary suffering for the tiny bitch and possibly heartbreak for the breeder. She should have some

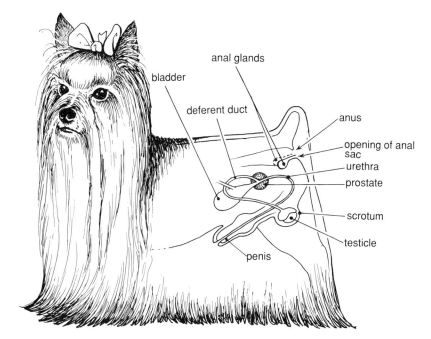

The male reproductive system.

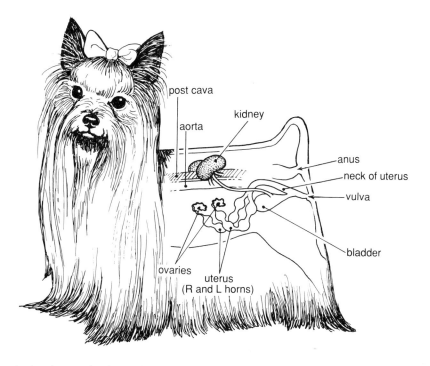

The female reproductive system.

141

quality breeding behind her, not necessarily a pedigree full of champions, although this could be an advantage.

The brood-bitch should be cared for in the same way as any other much-loved family pet and given exactly the same treatment. This means seeing to it that she receives regular exercise, a good diet and lots of love and attention; this is important as the bitch's temperament will be reflected in her puppies. The brood-bitch should enjoy life just like any other Yorkshire Terrier does, and not just be regarded as a puppy machine. Some people like to keep their brood-bitch in a short trim so that the coat does not get in the way when whelping or when rearing the puppies. I prefer this trim as it also makes it easier for bathing and grooming. Long hair can often cause problems, for instance, puppies have been known to get strangled in their mother's long hair. Other potential problems are that long hair can get in the way and hinder puppies from suckling, and long hair around the bitch's rear can sometimes make mating a little difficult for the stud-dog and should be either crackered up or trimmed shorter for the occasion. The only time there is a cause for special treatment for the brood-bitch, such as diet or special observation, is when she is in season or when she is pregnant, or of course, when she is unwell.

Bitch's Season

Generally bitches will come into season somewhere between the ages of six months and one year and most will have two seasons per year, but there are those who will only have one every twelve months. The season normally lasts about three weeks, during which time there will be several indications of her condition, starting with a swelling of the vulva accompanied by a deep-red discharge. This discharge will get progressively lighter in colour over the first ten or so days of the season.

The bitch may be mated from about the tenth day of the season; at this stage the discharge will probably be clear. From this point the swelling of the vulva will subside and the discharge slowly dry up until the season has passed, after approximately three weeks have elapsed. At the tenth or eleventh day the bitch will probably also indicate her readiness to mate by 'standing', and will turn her tail to the side when touched on her rear.

The author's Ch. Ozmilion Love Romance, dam to Ch. and Ir. Ch.
Ozmilion Sensation.

Mating

Although ready in season, some bitches may not accept the dog
mounting her straight away. She may be a maiden bitch and be
apprehensive and unsure of what is happening, which could lead to
her attacking the dog. The bitch must be firmly held whilst the dog is
mounting her; hold her under the neck and the head whilst supporting under the belly to prevent her from sitting down and frustrating
the dog's efforts. It is a good idea to have all matings supervised by
two people, one to hold the bitch and one to help the dog. Some dogs
will need assistance, especially if the bitch is larger than the dog, in
which case a thick book or rolled-up blanket for the dog to stand on
will help. If the bitch has a small vulva and the dog has difficulty
penetrating her then some form of lubricant such as petroleum jelly
should be used to ease his task.

Stud-dogs will vary greatly in both experience and temperament.
Some dogs are a little too eager and will charge around in a frantic
effort to mount the bitch. This type of dog will often not achieve

Feb	Dec	Jan	Nov	Dec	Oct	Nov	Sept	Oct	Aug	Sept	July	Aug	June	July	May	June	Apr	May	Mar	Apr	Feb	Mar	Jan
2	1	3	1	3	1	3	1	3	1	2	1	3	1	3	1	3	1	3	1	5	1	5	1
3	2	4	2	4	2	4	2	4	2	3	2	4	2	4	2	4	2	4	2	6	2	6	2
4	3	5	3	5	3	5	3	5	3	4	3	5	3	5	3	5	3	5	3	7	3	7	3
5	4	6	4	6	4	6	4	6	4	5	4	6	4	6	4	6	4	6	4	8	4	8	4
6	5	7	5	7	5	7	5	7	5	6	5	7	5	7	5	7	5	7	5	9	5	9	5
7	6	8	6	8	6	8	6	8	6	7	6	8	6	8	6	8	6	8	6	10	6	10	6
8	7	9	7	9	7	9	7	9	7	8	7	9	7	9	7	9	7	9	7	11	7	11	7
9	8	10	8	10	8	10	8	10	8	9	8	10	8	10	8	10	8	10	8	12	8	12	8
10	9	11	9	11	9	11	9	11	9	10	9	11	9	11	9	11	9	11	9	13	9	13	9
11	10	12	10	12	10	12	10	12	10	11	10	12	10	12	10	12	10	12	10	14	10	14	10
12	11	13	11	13	11	13	11	13	11	12	11	13	11	13	11	13	11	13	11	15	11	15	11
13	12	14	12	14	12	14	12	14	12	13	12	14	12	14	12	14	12	14	12	16	12	16	12
14	13	15	13	15	13	15	13	15	13	14	13	15	13	15	13	15	13	15	13	17	13	17	13
15	14	16	14	16	14	16	14	16	14	15	14	16	14	16	14	16	14	16	14	18	14	18	14
16	15	17	15	17	15	17	15	17	15	16	15	17	15	17	15	17	15	17	15	19	15	19	15
17	16	18	16	18	16	18	16	18	16	17	16	18	16	18	16	18	16	18	16	20	16	20	16
18	17	19	17	19	17	19	17	19	17	18	17	19	17	19	17	19	17	19	17	21	17	21	17
19	18	20	18	20	18	20	18	20	18	19	18	20	18	20	18	20	18	20	18	22	18	22	18
20	19	21	19	21	19	21	19	21	19	20	19	21	19	21	19	21	19	21	19	23	19	23	19
21	20	22	20	22	20	22	20	22	20	21	20	22	20	22	20	22	20	22	20	24	20	24	20
22	21	23	21	23	21	23	21	23	21	22	21	23	21	23	21	23	21	23	21	25	21	25	21
23	22	24	22	24	22	24	22	24	22	23	22	24	22	24	22	24	22	24	22	26	22	26	22
24	23	25	23	25	23	25	23	25	23	24	23	25	23	25	23	25	23	25	23	27	23	27	23
25	24	26	24	26	24	26	24	26	24	25	24	26	24	26	24	26	24	26	24	28	24	28	24
26	25	27	25	27	25	27	25	27	25	26	25	27	25	27	25	27	25	27	25	29	25	29	25
27	26	28	26	28	26	28	26	28	26	27	26	28	26	28	26	28	26	28	26	30	26	30	26
28	27	29	27	29	27	29	27	29	27	28	27	29	27	29	27	29	27	29	27	May 1	27	31	27
Mar 1	28	30	28	30	28	30	28	30	28	29	28	30	28	30	28	30	28	30	28	May 2	28	Apr 1	28
Mar 2	29	31	29	31	29	Dec 1	29	31	29	30	29	31	29	31	29	July 1	29	31	29			Apr 2	29
Mar 3	30	Feb 1	30	Jan 1	30	Dec 2	30	Nov 1	30	Oct 1	30	Sept 1	30	Aug 1	30	July 2	30	June 1	30			Apr 3	30
Mar 4	31			Jan 2	31			Nov 2	31	Oct 2	31			Aug 2	31			June 2	31			Apr 4	31

Welping Table.

penetration and will need to be restrained, calmed down and assisted and will need to be guided to penetration by the handlers supervising the mating. Other dogs are much calmer, sometimes even apprehensive about approaching the bitch because they have been bitten during a previous mating. The calmer dog will be much easier to mate and will be a good choice to pair with a maiden bitch, who may find the more excitable dog too much for her first experience. After the mating is completed the stud-dog should be put into an individual kennel or pen away from other dogs – he will be carrying the scent of the bitch and may well be involved in fighting if placed back with other males at this time. After a period of about five to ten minutes, check that the dog's penis has withdrawn into the sheath. If this has not happened, owing perhaps to some hair caught in the sheath or something similar, cold water should be applied to the area to assist retraction of the penis; a little lubricant may also assist. If this condition is not rectified a painful swelling may occur and the dog could become distressed, at which point, veterinary assistance should be sought.

Pre-Natal Care

It is not always easy to tell if a bitch has taken or not without having a vet examine her. Pregnancy can usually be confirmed by a vet about twenty-one days after mating, although nowadays there are advance testing kits which can test earlier than this. I prefer to wait and see, as sometimes a bitch may have a touch of morning sickness after about three weeks following the mating, or at a later date she may become exceptionally fussy about her food. Some bitches have the same tell-tale symptoms each time they are pregnant while with others the symptoms may vary. However, time will tell and Yorkshire Terriers are full of surprises.

It is a good idea to worm your bitch before you mate her or certainly no later than two weeks after the mating as failure to do this may affect the bitch and cause problems. She will need to be wormed again a week after you worm her puppies; this is normally from four weeks of age onwards depending on the product used.

Once the bitch has been mated, she should be treated as usual, no special attention is initially required but exercise is an important factor in order to keep the brood-bitch fit and healthy. Also a good balanced diet including high-quality protein and all the necessary vitamins should be provided; there is no need to give any extra calcium to the bitch at this stage. There is no immediate reason to increase the intake of food until about five weeks into the pregnancy when the expectant bitch should be fed on a high-protein diet consisting of two meals per day. It is not until the last ten days of her pregnancy that she should be given extra calcium when this can be given in the form of one of the many proprietary brands on the market.

False Pregnancy or Phantom Pregnancy

There are two types of false pregnancy, which is a condition where the bitch exhibits the signs of an expectant mother but is not actually pregnant – these signs may be physical or behavioural.

A bitch sometimes conceives and then absorbs her litter early in the pregnancy without having to abort. There are a number of reasons why this may occur, such as an environmental infection or a dietary deficiency.

The other type of false pregnancy occurs when the bitch did not conceive in the first place but carries on as if she is pregnant. This is the most common type of false pregnancy.

These bitches may show many signs of being pregnant such as collecting toys and other objects in their bedding or in another quiet place, they may even produce milk and in the most extreme cases may start straining and going through the motions of labour.

In non-extreme cases the removal of the various toys and objects without any special attention being paid to the bitch is the best course of action and usually she will return to her normal non-brooding self within a few days. Conversely, special attention and careful observation is needed when the bitch shows signs of producing milk; if it is a large quantity that is produced then it may lead to mastitis. At the very first signs of an enlarged mammary gland the bitch's exercise should be increased and her diet strictly controlled. Her diet should have a low carbohydrate level and she should have no milk, calcium or bones as these encourage the production of milk. One exception is where the breeder could use this milk-producing bitch to help rear some puppies from an over-sized litter that is too much for the natural mother to cope with herself.

Should a bitch be in a critical state because of her phantom pregnancy then the vet can help her with hormones. These can be given in the form of injections or tablets. If any bitch suffers particularly badly or on a regular basis then it is best to have her spayed if she is not to be bred from.

Overdue Pregnancy

Sometimes abnormalities do occur and the bitch may go over her time due for whelping in which case some intervention will be required. If it is more than two days overdue then it may be necessary for a vet to examine the bitch, though do remember to allow for a second mating (if the bitch was mated on two occasions) when working out the gestation period. It has been known for bitches to show no signs at all when really they should be going into labour. This is known as inertia. Inertia can result when a bitch has been having contractions for so long that the uterus has become exhausted, or the whelps are just too big for the mother to pass through her vulva. This can often go on unnoticed because the contractions are so weak and finally the bitch will give up. This is a job for the vet and will probably need a Caesarian if all else fails.

Premature Birth

Premature birth can also be a problem that has to be watched for. The more premature the birth the less hope there is for the puppies' survival. If the puppies arrive just a couple of days early or even up to one week early then with much effort the puppies may well survive. Should the puppies be delivered more than one week prematurely, the chances of survival are slim. If there is any possibility of a premature birth it is extremely important that you should constantly monitor a pregnant bitch for at least the last eight days before she is due to whelp. It is also advisable to let your vet know in advance that the mother is due to whelp soon so that you will be able to contact him easily when necessary.

Whelping

Prior to whelping it is a good idea to collect a selection of useful items which will be needed during the whelping period. These items

147

should be kept together in a suitable box or case ready for use. The following is a suggested list:

Petroleum Jelly
Thermometer
Scissors – these should have a serrated edge for cutting the cord.
Pair of forceps
Oral syringe or teaspoon for giving liquid calcium
Needle (sterile)
Liquid calcium such as Calo Cal D
Hand basin
Hand towels (several towels for rubbing the puppies immediately after they are born to stimulate circulation); a separate towel to assist holding the puppy during a breech birth.
Length of cotton (for tying umbilical cord)
Cotton wool
A calcium supplement for the bitch
Heat pad or infra-red lamp
Small bottle of alcohol or surgical spirit
Surgical gloves.

The expectant bitch should be acclimatized to her intended whelping place by putting her there for a short time each day during the last two weeks before her whelping date. I prefer to use a proper whelping pen which I allow the pregnant bitch to sleep in every night during the two weeks prior to whelping. This enables her to become accustomed to it. I always put a small blanket or special doggy bedding in the whelping box for the bitch to sleep on but this will be taken out and replaced by newspapers when the bitch is actually whelping because newspapers are better at this stage. They help the bitch by giving her something to scratch while she is having labour pains and do not hinder her while working on her puppies. I am always afraid a tiny puppy may suffocate under a blanket, so I keep my puppies and nursing bitch on newspapers for the first two weeks following the whelping.

The whelping pen should not be in a cold, damp or draughty place and a heat pad or a heat lamp should be used to keep the little family warm, though there should not be too much heat as this will cause the bitch to pant and be uncomfortable. The pen should be in a quiet place where the bitch will not be distracted while whelping or nursing her young, but at the same time it should not be too far out of sight that you cannot hear or attend in the case of a problem.

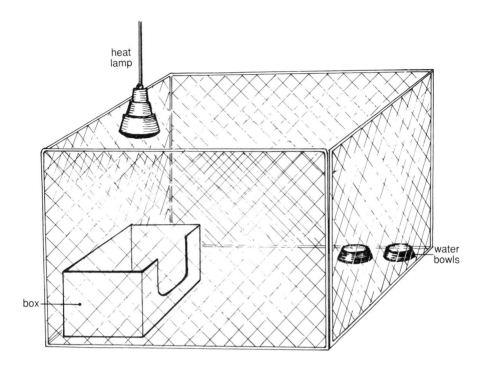

Whelping box.

The Normal Birth

The normal gestation period is sixty-three days following a successful mating, although some expectant bitches will whelp from around fifty-nine days onwards, some may even go as long as sixty-five days but should not be allowed to exceed this period without seeking veterinary advice.

Just prior to whelping the bitch will start to act differently, perhaps becoming more affectionate and trying to be with you all the time demanding your attention, though behaviour patterns can vary from one bitch to another. Maiden bitches tend to be a little more apprehensive about the whole thing and may also be afraid, so the bitch will be much more at ease if you are present while she is going through this difficult stage. Place the expectant mother in a dog pen with a strong cardboard box or whelping box inside. Ensure that the bitch has sufficient room to move around and on no account allow the practice of jumping in or out of the pen as this could cause damage or complications. Once she starts to go into labour, it is important to keep an eye on her in case she requires assistance. Never allow her to hide under a bed or inside a cupboard.

On the day of whelping the bitch may refuse food, but this is not a clear indication as it is not uncommon for a bitch to eat a meal and then go into labour shortly afterwards. Because of their condition a lot of bitches go on and off their food quite frequently while they are pregnant; this is something you will have to be aware of and make allowance for.

A drop in the bitch's temperature to 99°F (37°C) may be noticed but this can happen a day or so before the whelping time and should not cause alarm. Also at this time it may be noticed that the bitch has begun to produce milk. A sure sign of labour is when the bitch starts scratching frantically in her box, and may also cry and yelp. Usually she will be lying on her side although a few bitches may stand up and contract. You must watch the bitch carefully and make a note of the time of the first signs of contractions; this will be important in deciding if it is necessary to call the vet in. Once the contractions have started you should gently stroke the bitch and reassure her by talking to her calmly. Be sure to leave her in the box all the time. While she is scratching around the bitch may start to pant and strain, she may stand up and lie down again and move from one end of the box to the other looking very restless and generally uncomfortable. Offer her a drink of warm milk but only a small amount if she will accept it. Eventually the bitch, while lying on her side or standing arch-backed, will put her head down and lift her tail a few times as she contracts, then after a few contractions and hard straining the water bag will be passed, this will be followed in due course by the whelp (puppy) covered in a shiny bag of transparent membrane. This must be broken on arrival in order for the whelp to breathe and will normally be done by the new dam herself. Normally she will clean the whelp herself and sever the umbilical cord that connects them together. If the bitch is a maiden bitch and seems a little bewildered by it all and is a little slow to act, then you will have no choice but to intervene. This is explained in greater detail later in this chapter. The bitch will now eat the placenta (afterbirth). I prefer to let the bitch eat only one or two of these as any more can create digestive problems, so you should throw away the rest. While the bitch is occupied with the placenta you should clean and dry the puppy with a towel and stimulate it by massaging and rubbing to encourage it to breathe.

Puppies normally arrive at intervals of twenty or thirty minutes but if it takes a little longer there is no need to be concerned. Should she continue to strain and have contractions for more than two hours then you should assist her. If she is relaxed, lying comfortably and looking after her new puppies without panting, lifting her tail or straining, she has probably finished whelping. Once the bitch has finished giving birth, you may offer her a warm drink of milk mixed with a raw egg yolk and a pinch of glucose powder. A dose of Calo Cal D calcium supplement (1ml per 4½ pounds (2kg) of bodyweight per day) would be recommended at this point but be careful not to give too much as this is as bad as giving none at all.

Remember, even if all goes well it is still a good practice to let your vet give the bitch a thorough check over some time after she has settled down. This is normally done at the time when the vet is docking the puppies' tails.

When to Call the Vet

Once the water bag has been passed the puppies could follow at any time, but in a case where several hours elapse the vet should be alerted, as some stimulation may be required by the bitch. In the case where the bitch has passed the water bag and continues straining for some time without any result, do not waste too much time as there may well be a complication. Some may disagree, but I personally will not wait more than two hours before calling the vet.

Complications

Breech Birth

A breech birth is the presentation of a puppy the wrong way around. This means the hind feet arrive first instead of the head first and this can cause a problem for the bitch, especially if the puppy is a large one. This type of birth may require some help, especially if the water bag on the puppy has broken, when every moment counts. You must grasp the hind leg with a handkerchief or piece of cloth as the puppies are very slippery, do not let go at this stage as the puppy will go back inside the birth canal and is likely to drown or suffocate. Wait for the bitch to contract and as she does so pull the puppy in a

151

downwards direction towards the bitch. Be sure to pull only when there are contractions.

Having helped the gasping puppy it should be put back with its mum. Whilst assisting a breech birth you may need to lubricate the bitch's vulva with some petroleum jelly. Be sure to get the afterbirth out at the same time as the puppy. Some bitches may only have one breech birth with the rest of the litter being delivered normally; other mothers may have every puppy as a breech birth, so be prepared for the next one. Assistance may be required by the breeder in the case of a breech birth so a friend or companion should be at hand to help at all times when a litter is being born. This is a great help especially if one needs to go to the vet (it helps if one of you can drive).

Another possible problem is that the puppy may be coming out as a breech birth but may be having a problem getting his shoulders out. In this case you must lend some assistance by gently moving the puppy from side to side until his shoulders are released.

In the case where the breeder has to intervene and sever the umbilical cord, it is important that you do not use straight-edged scissors as these make a clean cut which may cause haemorrhaging. Start half-way between the puppy and the afterbirth. Tie off the cord with a length of cotton thread and with a sterile pair of serrated-edged scissors, cut below the tied cotton or tear the cord using your finger nails (provided your hands and nails are sterile). This way there should not be any bleeding. If this method is used, it is important that the cord is pulled from the direction of the placenta towards the puppy, *never* in the opposite direction as this may damage the puppy. Pay special attention to the mum once you have returned the puppy as some mothers tend to become over concerned with the cord and may do considerable harm to the puppy (this is more likely with a first-time mother). Once you have severed the cord, dry the puppy with a towel; do not worry about being a little vigorous in doing this as this will help stimulate the newborn.

In the case of a gasping puppy whose delivery had been delayed, there is the possibility that it has taken some fluid into its lungs. Gently supporting the puppy's body with a hand, and holding its head firmly with your thumb and index finger hold the puppy upside down for ten seconds then bring it back up. You should wipe away any fluid from its nostrils, then blow very gently down its nose and repeat the above procedure until the puppy is breathing comfortably. Once the puppy is breathing easily you should wipe it over with the towel and place it back with its dam.

The Retained Puppy or Whelp

It can sometimes be difficult to know whether or not there are any more puppies left in the uterus or if the whelping is finally completed. Sometimes, feeling the uterus gives the impression that there is a retained whelp; this is because the uterus swells up quite a lot after the whelping has finished. If the uterus is gently and carefully felt immediately after each puppy is delivered it may be easier to assess the possibility of further whelps before the uterus swells up. When a puppy is retained it can be very dangerous indeed as this causes very serious infection and could kill the bitch if left. Again this is another good reason for the vet to see the bitch after her whelping (ideally as soon after whelping as possible). If there is a puppy still retained then the vet can give a pituitary extract injection to cause the bitch to contract and deliver the puppy. The delivery must be closely supervised. Should the injection fail, then a Caesarean section must be performed to remove the puppy from the mother's uterus.

Retained Afterbirth

Afterbirths retained by the bitch can be extremely dangerous as this can cause septicaemia. In order to prevent unnecessary infection keep a track of the number of afterbirths produced and if one is still left inside, get the vet to give an injection of pituitary extract in order to make the bitch's uterus contract and expel the afterbirth. The vet will probably also give some penicillin to the bitch in the case of any infection from the retained afterbirth.

Caesarian Section

There are a number of reasons why a pregnant bitch may have to have a Caesarian section performed. Fortunately nowadays this operation is usually carried out quite successfully by the vet who should only resort to it if there is no other way of delivering the puppies. In order to perform the operation the mother must first have an anaesthetic and it is very important that you monitor both the mother and her puppies for any after-effects of this. When the mother begins to come around from the anaesthetic she will be quite unsteady and you must take care to see that she does not fall or lie on the puppies and suffocate them. Some breeders like to take the puppies away until the mother is completely back to normal, but this sometimes causes distress to the bitch and further damage can be done through the bitch's attempts to seek her newborn puppies. I personally prefer to stay close by and keep the puppies with their dam. It is essential that the bitch and her puppies are kept clean and warm and out of any draughts, but on the other hand too much heat will cause the bitch discomfort.

A drink of warm milk can be offered to the bitch as soon as she is comfortable and back to her normal self. A routine check should be made to the bitch's abdomen to see if all is well with the stitches. Sometimes a slight swelling may be observed around the stitches which is not uncommon and is no reason for alarm, unless the swelling is great or pus is present, in which case it is best to get the vet to look at the area. If all is well, then the bitch will have to see the vet in ten days' time in order to remove the stitches.

Occasionally a bitch may neglect her puppies when she comes around from the anaesthetic. This is more likely with a first-time mother who wakes up to the sound of squeaking puppies who are crawling around her. Time and patience is required by the breeder in order to help the bitch. Wiping the afterbirth over the puppies before disposing of it, or expelling some of the bitch's milk onto them, may encourage the mother to clean her offspring thus forming a bond between mum and puppies. Normally with a little assistance from the breeder the new mother will accept her puppies.

It is important and necessary for a healthy bitch's body that the puppies start to feed and suckle from her. In the early days after the operation it is also important to keep a close eye on the bitch to see that she does not jump or move around too fast as this can do damage to the area where her stitches are and she could require restitching if she has not been carefully looked after. For the first few days the new mother should be fed on a light diet consisting of a small amount of food fed frequently. She should also be given warm drinks occasionally.

Eclampsia (Milk Fever)

A low calcium level in the bitch's blood is the cause of this condition which normally occurs in the first three weeks of lactation, when there is a strong drain on the bitch's calcium store. This affects mainly toy breeds and particularly those with large litters of strong healthy puppies. Too much heat and stress can also contribute to eclampsia especially in a young bitch's first litter.

The first signs are persistent panting and rapid breathing followed by trembling of the hind legs. The bitch is generally quite restless, possibly whining and pacing up and down. It is important at this stage to get her to the vet for an intravenous calcium injection in order to restore her calcium level. If not treated, the bitch will eventually become shaky and collapse on her side almost fighting for life. Fast action must be taken in order to save her. In severe cases the bitch may not be able to return to her puppies for some time, if at all, after her treatment, so the puppies will require supplementary feeding. The vet will advise whether or not the mum can be returned to her babies and if so she may need to be supervised and only allowed to return for five minutes or so several times a day and night.

Be sure to maintain the calcium, as it is not uncommon for a bitch to have more than one attack in a short space of time. The vet should be able to tell you what steps to take and whether or not to breed from the bitch again, as most breeders normally do not.

As with most health aspects, prevention is better than cure, and in the case of preventing eclampsia it is important to ensure that the expectant bitch receives higher-than-normal levels of calcium during the last fortnight of her pregnancy.

Mastitis

This is a condition normally associated with lactating bitches and usually occurs within the first few days following whelping. The bitch, possibly having a small litter of puppies, can sometimes overproduce milk and as the milk is not being taken by the puppies, the mammary glands tend to become rather swollen and lumpy.

If found in the early stages, the breeder can put the puppies on to the affected teat to feed, thus reducing the quantity of milk. But if the glands have already become very hard and produce very thick milk, the puppies may not accept this milk as it may have gone a little sour, and could make the puppies sick. If this is the case, use a clean cloth and very warm water (not hot) and gently start to massage the affected area, which is normally the hind teats, gently squeezing out some of the milk. Do this about twice a day until she is back to her usual condition.

Remember that this may be painful for the mum and she may need a little comforting. A little olive oil may also be put on to help relieve the soreness. In a severe case of mastitis the vet may need to be called and the bitch may have to have a course of antibiotics. Whilst in this condition the bitch's intake of milk and calcium should be reduced. Failure to help the mum may cause further problems.

Acute Metritis (Infection of the Uterus)

Acute metritis is an infection that spreads up through the birth canal during the delivery of puppies or immediately afterwards. It affects the lining of the uterus and can occur if part of the afterbirth (placenta) has not been expelled, or a retained foetus has mummified. Acute metritis can also occur as a result of contamination of the birth canal caused by the use of non-sterile instruments or fingers during difficulties in labour. Symptoms include depression, refusal of food and a high temperature accompanied by a dark, bloody, greenish discharge, excessive thirst and possibly vomiting and diarrhoea. It is therefore advisable to have your vet give your bitch a thorough check over. He may wish to give the bitch an injection or a course of antibiotics just to be sure.

Fading Puppies

It is not uncommon and normally no fault of the breeder when one or more of the puppies starts aimlessly crawling around while constantly whining and screaming, and so causing distress to its mother. The puppy will have very little interest in feeding and so will dehydrate very quickly, and a yellow diarrhoea will appear on the puppy or around the bedding. The lack of interest in the puppy by the mother soon becomes apparent and this is the time for you to take over. Set aside a place in another room away from the mother and the rest of the litter, and start to hand-feed the puppy, (*see* pages 157–9 on hand-rearing). This is a very time-consuming task and is not always successful. If your efforts are successful then the puppy can soon be returned to its mother and its progress monitored.

Fading puppy syndrome is normally a E-Coli infection and a course of antibiotics may be needed. The vet may also wish to inject the puppy in order to stimulate feeding. Although it is normally the weaker puppies that are affected with fading puppy syndrome, sometimes the stronger ones can go down as well. As the bug takes hold in the puppy it may change from a fat and healthy little puppy to a disturbed and whining puppy within a short period of time.

Besides E-Coli bacteria there are other possible causes of fading puppy syndrome. It could be that they are getting no nourishment as the mother's milk has not yet come through.

Another possibility is the mother having deformed nipples from which the puppy cannot suckle, also the puppy may have a handicap such as harelip or cleft palate. In order to foresee and deal with these types of problem it is most important for the novice breeder to have a vet check over all the puppies and the mother as soon as possible.

Hand-Rearing

Every breeders' nightmare is the possibility of losing a beloved companion through whelping. Besides the upset of losing the mother you will be left to rear the puppies by hand. In the lucky event that the breeder may have another bitch with puppies at the time or may know of one not too far away, then the trauma of hand-feeding the babies is made simpler by the substitute mother. However, if there is no other alternative, the job of hand-rearing the puppies must start.

Firstly the puppies should be put into a warm box with a heat pad under them, or a heat lamp safely suspended over them, as it is very important that the puppies should be kept warm at all times and at a constant temperature. At this stage they have little or no body temperature control. The puppies can actually survive longer without food than without warmth and so it is most important that the air temperature should be kept at a constant 95–100°F (35–37.8°C). To monitor this keep a thermometer in the box with the babies and check it regularly. You should weigh each puppy at birth and make a note of this weight and then weigh the puppies regularly at least twice daily for the first two weeks to make sure the puppies are gaining weight. All feeding equipment used should be cleaned regularly and so should the puppies' living quarters. It is best to keep the babies away from all strangers and other dogs. Remember if the puppies have not fed from their mother's milk they will not have received any passive immunity and therefore they are susceptible to many diseases and especially viruses. Because of this special vaccinations should be administered when the puppies are three weeks old.

Feeding the Orphan Puppies

There are a variety of specially formulated dried milks available that are made specially for the hand-rearing of puppies and kittens. I state this, as these contain particular vitamins and other essentials that are required by these infants. There are also puppy and kitten foster feeding bottles available with the adequate sized nipples. Alternatively, a syringe or a dropper could be used to feed the young puppies. If a special hand-rearing milk is not available then goat's milk or tinned milk can be used. When using tinned milk it should be mixed as three parts water to four parts milk. Whichever milk is used the puppy will require about two tablespoons or so of fluid. When using the dried milk make the mixture as directed on the packet, just as you would when mixing for a human baby. It is important to ensure that the milk is fed to the puppies at a fairly warm temperature, at least blood temperature. If the liquid is too cold you may find that the puppies refuse to drink it, even though they may be very hungry. Start to feed the puppies as soon as is possible, you must feed slowly and carefully so as not to choke them. Feed one drop at a time and begin by placing one drop on the puppy's tongue when giving the very first feed. Some puppies have a little difficulty in suckling at first and so patience is required by the person feeding them.

The puppies will require feeding every three hours through both day and night while premature puppies will need feeding every two hours. It is very important to encourage the babies to urinate and defecate. This can be done by gently massaging the abdomen and anus with a piece of cotton wool moistened in warm water. This encouragement should follow after every feed as the puppies are unable to do this for themselves until they are three weeks old or so. Failure to do this for the puppy can lead to severe problems, like constipation or diarrhoea. Sometimes if a puppy will not feed and is crying and has a hard tummy, it may be constipated and need help to relieve the constipation.

Provided the puppies are having enough to fill them up they will rest from one feed to another. If the puppies are not being fed correctly and are receiving too much feed they will cry and their motion passed will become a yellow or a grey colour. If they are not receiving enough feed then their tummies will look flat and wrinkled and they will cry and crawl around in search of their mother. When feeding the puppies you should wrap a small towel around each which will help keep the front legs out of the way. The towel also acts as a bib to stop any liquid getting on the puppy's body and making it sticky and dirty. If this does happen you can clean the puppy up with warm damp cotton wool. It would probably be an idea to put the puppy in a separate box after feeding as each Yorkshire Terrier puppy looks like the other and you must make sure that every puppy has its feed. All infants can be returned back to the box together once the feeding is over.

Post-Natal Care

If all is well during the first few weeks the mother will look after her own puppies, cleaning and feeding them with devotion. You should keep a check on the new mum and her puppies many times during the day just to see that everything is fine. The proud mother will not want to leave her new young at first, but for her own good she must be encouraged to do so. You will have to put her out for a five-minute period a few times each day. This time apart should be increased as the puppies grow older.

The mother gives off her body heat to help keep the puppies warm and the puppies will cry and whinge if they are cold or uncomfortable. Supplementary heat may be required, but too much heat can cause discomfort for the mum. At about two weeks of age the puppies' eyes should open. They sometimes require a little assistance and the breeder can gently wipe the eyes with a piece of cotton wool that has been dipped in warm water. A separate piece of cotton wool must be used for each eye. It does not often happen, but if the puppies have a problem and the eyes do not open around the expected time you may need to seek advice from your vet. Around the same time as the eyes open the ears should open too.

Once the puppies start to stumble around, at about three weeks of age, the time has arrived to begin weaning them. They will also need their nails trimmed as their tiny sharp nails will cause discomfort to the bitch whilst her puppies continue suckling. It should take about two weeks before the puppies are taking all their food from a plate and not relying on their mother's milk.

From now on keep a check on the puppies' bottoms as sometimes it is necessary to give them a little wash as they tend to get a little caked up, especially if their mum has not been doing her job properly. After washing the bottom put a little petroleum jelly on it, just to help prevent it from becoming sore and causing discomfort.

The puppies can be wormed from around three weeks using the correct worm syrup. I normally worm my puppies at five weeks unless there is any other reason to do so beforehand.

Besides seeing that the puppies are well you should also pay attention to the new mother. You should check on her regularly to ensure she is coping with motherhood. You must be sure she is feeding her young as this will reduce the risk of complications. Sometimes bitches become very awkward to feed after giving birth to their puppies and therefore require encouragement and attention in order to get them to take food or drink. I personally like to feed boiled chicken in some of its own juices while it is still warm, about twice a day, and a little warm milk two or three times a day for the first few weeks. You may find that after this time the bitch may not be so fussy about her food and can be returned to her usual high-protein diet while she is nursing her young.

Tail Docking

Tail docking can be quite a controversial topic. There are many different views on the subject and a lot of vets will refuse to do it nowadays. Normally the operation is performed when the puppy is just a few days old. Although it is quite a small operation it can go very wrong if it is not carried out in a confident and hygienic manner by someone who knows exactly what they are doing. If a tail is to be docked then it must be done the proper way and in a certain place. This is especially true if the puppy is considered to be a potential show specimen, although it is perfectly acceptable to show Yorkshire Terriers with their tails left undocked.

Dew-Claws

These are the small single claws found a little way up on the inside of the front legs and they sometimes appear on the back legs as well. Normally all dew-claws should be removed at the same time as the puppies' tails are docked. If the dew-claws are not removed properly, they can often grow back again in a deformed-looking way.

A Yorkshire Terrier with dew-claws left in place may encounter various problems as they start to grow. The most common problem is that the nails on the dew-claws tend to get long and curled and can grow into the dog's leg where they can be very uncomfortable and painful. This is because, unlike the nails on the feet which will wear down through general exercise, the dew-claws never get used, and so

*Vic Chiswell with his Ch.
Chandas Shaunas Girl as a
puppy.*

if forgotten about and not regularly trimmed they will cause problems. The dew-claws may also get caught on clothing or carpet and
be pulled out, thus causing a lot of bleeding and pain to the dog.

Homing the Puppies

This is a difficult time for most breeders as there are many
considerations regarding where the puppies should start their
lives. In the case of very tiny puppies one must be sure that they
are going to a suitable home and environment. As the tiny ones at
this stage can be very delicate they may not adjust well to other
larger dogs or to boisterous young children in a very active
household. This can also prove fatal, particularly if the family is
not used to having tiny dogs around. Time must be spent with the
potential owner to be sure they are suitable and many things must
be pointed out to them.

You must take it upon yourself to decide whether or not this person is suitable to love and care for the puppies you have lovingly
brought up and cared for over the past weeks. The person must be
able to provide a puppy with its regular four meals a day. Therefore

it is not a good idea to let a puppy go to a home where it is to be left for the whole day while the family is out at work; this would be a bad start in life for a puppy who has just left its mum and brothers and sisters. It will need entertaining and training or it will probably sleep all day and spend the whole night crying causing distress to the new family and neighbours. Left alone it may become bored and do damage to furniture because it is not getting the attention it needs.

It can also occur that a puppy may be unwanted by its new owners at a later date and they wish to seek another home for the puppy. Since this is beyond your control, it is a good idea to mention to the new owners that you would want the puppy back if, at any time in the future, unforeseen circumstances dictate that they must find a new home for the puppy or adult Yorkshire Terrier.

A diet sheet should accompany the puppy stating what you have been feeding it on. If this was a complete puppy food then you should provide enough to last a few days and inform the new owners of where they can obtain this feed. As already stated in this book it is imperative that you stress to the new owners the importance of the vaccinations and any dietary supplement it may require. As a breeder, being selective with where you place your puppies and taking time to assist the new owners can only help to give you a good reputation. Because of this some breeders never have to advertise their puppies owing to the regular recommendations they get from vets, other breeders and very importantly, satisfied customers.

Breeders who produce stock for further breeding or for the show arena will usually advertise in the specialist dog press, whereas other breeders will usually advertise locally. A few breeders will sell their puppies to dealers or pet shops but most concerned breeders will avoid this as they cannot be sure where the puppies will finally end up. Normally when a breeder has used a well-known professional stud-dog then the stud-dog's owner may well pass on enquiries to him as this is a good advertisement for his own dog. Whichever method of placing your puppies you use, your concern should be that the placement is right for the puppy and that money alone should not determine its fate.

Export

Breeders' reactions to exporting their dogs and stock can vary considerably. Some will not export at all regardless of the destination as

The author's Ch. and Ir. Ch. Ozmilion Modesty.

they cannot be sure of their dog's future. Other breeders may export if they know the person they are letting the dogs go to. In the case of the top kennels, it is sometimes necessary to export in order to promote good stock around the world.

It is pleasing for a breeder to export a young dog to a breeder friend who will then show the dog in his own country and achieve success; also this will help that country's stock when he is used in breeding. When approached by a stranger from overseas who wishes to purchase one of your dogs, it is an idea to ask the potential buyer to supply you with photos of the dogs he already owns and where and how he keeps his dogs. If you then decide to part with one of your little companions and are satisfied with who is going to be the new owner, you should insist that he should personally come and collect the new addition to his family and, of course, you will assist him where you can. If the person is genuine he will be more than happy to collect the dog, thus getting an insight into the dog's home life and surroundings which will help him in settling the new dog into his own home.

7

Ailments and Diseases

In this chapter we will discuss some of the more common ailments and diseases that a Yorkshire Terrier may encounter. It is by no means an exhaustive study and neither is it meant for your own diagnosis of your pet's illnesses or complaints. Only with a breeder's many years of experience can some, and only some, of a dog's health problems be accurately diagnosed, and even then in some situations the only course of action will be to seek the vet's opinion and assistance. It is important that owners and breeders have a good relationship with their local vet as even the healthiest of dogs will need to visit him occasionally for booster vaccinations.

In many respects a sick dog is like a sick baby: we have to watch for changes in their behaviour or physical signs, and we cannot ask them what is wrong as we would an older child or adult. It may be obvious that your pet is not himself or that he is seriously ill, in which case you should get him to a vet as soon as possible. However, not all illnesses are obvious and if you do suspect or fear your dog is ill then you should seek the vet's diagnosis and assistance. It is always better to be safe than sorry in health matters.

Just as with humans there are a variety of complaints a dog can suffer from and these can be generally grouped as viruses or diseases, parasites or skin problems, or finally, injuries.

Distemper

Distemper is no longer as widespread as it once was but epidemics can still occur and it is very important that dogs are immunized against it. Distemper is a virus that damages the nervous system and can be fatal if not treated; even after recovering, an infected dog can have recurring problems later in his life. Dogs can become infected through other dogs or from sniffing around infected items such as blankets and clothing, when the virus enters the body through the dog's mucous membranes and attacks the nervous system.

164

The early signs of distemper are similar to those of a cold – the dog will have a runny nose, streaming eyes and possibly a cough. Also present will be a high temperature and vomiting. As the attack on the nervous system takes hold, the victim will begin to twitch. These twitches could be at any part of the body and if the dog is not treated will become more intense and frequent and eventually result in the dog having a fit. Ultimately they will prove fatal. In all cases a vet must be consulted.

Besides seeing to it that the puppy is inoculated at an early age and kept inside until he is protected in this way, do be sure to see that the adult dog is given his annual booster each and every year.

Parvovirus

It was in the latter part of 1978 that a new and dangerous disease, known to vets and breeders as parvovirus, was first discovered in Great Britain, North America, Australia and in Europe. This disease is closely related to the cat's disease feline infectious enteritis or feline panleucopaenia. The virus attacks and weakens the dog's natural immune system, therefore leaving the puppy entirely vulnerable to other diseases which can prove fatal.

Often there is very little warning that the dog has contracted the virus – this is particularly true of puppies, who in the early days of the discovery of this disease had no resistance at all. Puppies from as young as three weeks old would suddenly become extremely ill and die shortly afterwards, the virus often causing a high death rate among the litter of puppies. The actual cause of these deaths was diagnosed as inflammation of the heart muscles brought on by the virus.

With older dogs the effects of the virus may take longer to become apparent and usually lead to gastro-enteritis which can prove fatal due to dehydration. The infected dog may show many signs of being ill which may include a general listlessness, a lethargic manner, foul-smelling diarrhoea mixed with some blood, vomiting possibly mixed with blood, uncoordinated body movements and a keen interest in his water bowl without actually drinking from it.

Fortunately good vaccines have been developed now and these are given to young puppies in their initial series of immunization by the vet, so giving a high level of resistance to parvovirus. However, should any dog show the symptoms described then the vet's assistance should be sought in much haste.

Leptospirosis

Here we are concerned with two bacterial diseases namely leptospiral jaundice and leptospiral nephritis.

These viruses are carried in the urine of rats. Leptospirosis is a disease that can be passed on to humans and is then commonly known as Weil's disease. Just like human's, dogs contract this from almost any association with rats, such as contaminated drinking water, ponds, canals and their surrounding areas, also on farms where there may be a heavy population of rats. All puppies are normally vaccinated against this in their initial course of vaccinations.

The symptoms of this disease are a high temperature, abdominal pains, frequent urinating, severe thirst, ulcerations of the mouth, vomiting, diarrhoea and jaundice. Most urgent veterinary attention is required as this is a very infectious disease and constant attention to hygiene is necessary to prevent the infection spreading to other dogs. A dog that recovers from leptospirosis may encounter serious kidney problems later on in life.

Hepatitis

Canine infectious hepatitis is a highly contagious disease and has no connection to the human strain of hepatitis. Dogs can be infected by immediate contact with saliva, faeces or the urine of an infected dog. Again puppies are protected through their initial inoculations. Generally the younger dogs are more at risk but dogs of all ages are susceptible to hepatitis.

Symptoms are similar to those of leptospirosis. Often dogs recovering from hepatitis may have a blue film over their eyes for a short period of time after their recovery. Only veterinary assistance can help infected animals and the strictest hygiene is necessary to help control the spread of the infection. This is necessary as infected animals will shed the infection through their urine and the virus can survive for some time afterwards.

After the initial course of vaccination given to puppies, regular yearly booster vaccinations should be administered to all dogs in order to control all the above-mentioned viruses.

Kennel Cough

Kennel cough is a highly contagious respiratory problem, and a dog must be injected against it as soon as it is diagnosed. This illness owes its name to the fact that dogs usually contract the illness while in kennels. This problem arises when the dogs are left to bark unnecessarily. If your dog has to go into a kennel it would be best for him to have the injection before he goes as it will give him some protection although total immunity is not guaranteed.

Once contracted, the cough is very harsh and dry and becomes worse at night. The dog will look healthy and will probably still have a normal appetite. When it is a mild case you must segregate the dog from the other dogs. With some moderate exercise and vitamins added to his diet the cough should disappear in a couple of weeks. Should your dog contract a severe case of kennel cough then more action is required. Again the dog should be isolated from other dogs to reduce the risk of infecting others and the dog should get plenty of rest and have added vitamins in his diet. He will also need to have an injection through his nose which would be given by the vet. In addition, as this is a contagious disease and can travel through the air, even to another room, all the dog's bedding and utensils must be disinfected and kept clean. To combat these airborne germs a humidifier should be used and the air cleansed by use of a disinfectant air spray. With this treatment your dog should make a gradual recovery.

Fleas

Fleas are probably the most common form of parasite found on dogs. Fleas live in the coat and feed on the animal's blood. Infestation can often be seen as a 'salt and pepper' effect on the coat. The salt being the flea eggs and the pepper being the flea excrement, which is blackish in colour; both are about the size of grains of sand. The fleas themselves can be seen moving around the dog's belly, chest and neck or even around his anus or base of tail. The dog is likely to scratch a lot and be generally restless and irritable. A good insecticidal shampoo will rid the animal of the fleas and eggs, but it must be remembered that the dog's bedding must be sprayed with insecticidal spray and all carpets around the area should be regularly vacuumed to pick up any eggs.

Fleas flourish in a warm, humid environment. They are most

common in the summer but do also occur in the winter. They will obviously be found all the year round on animals kept in the home, where the eggs will incubate in the carpets and furniture. High standards of cleanliness and hygiene are important in the fight against fleas. It is important to keep fleas down as heavy infestation can reduce a healthy animal to a mess in no time at all.

Ear Mites

Ear mites live in the dog's ear canal and feed on the debris and detritus which collects therein. They cannot be seen with the naked eye but show up under strong magnification. A dog with an ear mite infection will scratch his ears repeatedly, shake his head and may hold it to one side, also a 'sploshing' sound may be heard if the area under the ear is rubbed. Do not be tempted to probe around in the ear if you suspect an ear mite problem.

Ear mites are very mobile and will quickly infect both ears on an animal and any other animals which come into contact with the infected host. The usual treatment is a course of ear drops over several days. Any excess hair in the dog's ears should be plucked out.

Skin Problems

Sarcoptic Mange

Sarcoptic mange or scabies, to give it its common name, is a disease caused by a minute spider-like creature and will cause intense itching. This irritation is most pronounced while the female mite is burrowing into the host's skin to lay her eggs which will hatch within a very short period of time. The complete life cycle of this mite is about seventeen days or so.

Symptoms may be first noticed around the elbows, legs, face and ears. The infected dog will suffer from very irritating, rusty skin which, when touched, will cause the dog to scratch the area. Itchy, red bumps like insect bites may appear and sometimes these will form weepy patches. A special shampoo from your vet will be necessary to help relieve the dog of this irritating mite. This mite can also live on humans, but only for a short time.

Cheyletiella Mange (Walking Dandruff)

This complaint is most common in Yorkshire Terrier puppies and is recognizable by the vast amounts of what appears to be dandruff over the head, neck and shoulders of the puppy and, in severe cases, all over the puppy's body. This can also be very irritating to humans, causing small, white itchy bumps to form on the skin which has been in contact with the infected puppy; this will only last a few hours or so.

Various insecticidal shampoos are available and these will rid the puppy of the mite responsible but a thorough clean out of bedding, kennels, and so forth, with an insecticidal type of disinfectant must be carried out as this mite can be harboured in the environment and will reappear again and again. When treating the puppy be aware that the insecticidal shampoo may be very powerful so be sure to read the instructions carefully and avoid contact with the eyes and mouth. While the puppy is lathered up with the shampoo gently comb him through as this will increase its effectiveness. This mite is highly contagious and other dogs or puppies may also need treating.

Ringworm

This is an infection of the skin and not a worm as its name implies. It is a growth that lives on the surface of the dog's skin and is normally caused by a fungus. This fungus is circle-like in appearance and will rapidly spread on the body. Although this is not an itchy condition, scabs can form and sometimes weep. The circular patches which are formed by ringworm can vary in size from 1–1½ inches (2–4cm). In severe cases ringworm can be transmitted to humans and other animals so special attention should be paid to the hygiene and segregation of infected animals. While administering treatment to an infected dog rubber gloves should be worn to protect the hands. Children seem to be more susceptible than adults.

Ringworm is generally associated with bad living conditions although infection can occur through open wounds coming into contact with infected ground. Any person suspecting their dog of having ringworm must seek veterinary advice as various tests on the dog's skin must be carried out before one can be certain.

Demodectic Mange

Demodectic mange, also known as *Demodex canis*, is another tiny mite that attacks the skin but will only do so if they exist in sufficient quantity. Most dogs have these mites living on their skin without causing any problems, but sometimes, they will multiply, breaking down the dog's natural resistance to them. This is a more common problem in short-haired dogs and normally affects younger dogs in their first year. The early signs of this complaint include hair loss around eyes and mouth giving an almost moth-eaten appearance. Sometimes the loss of hair around the front legs will cause patchiness, possibly giving an impression of ringworm but this will only last a few months if treated correctly. If the condition is allowed to progress causing much larger patches of hair loss on the head, legs and body, sores and scabs may then occur and create a very uncomfortable condition for the dog. The treatment for this condition must be administered under veterinary supervision.

Lice

Lice or nits are not a common problem amongst well-kept dogs in good condition. Lice feed on the skin scales and on the dog's blood. Owing to their minute size, lice can only be seen through a magnifying glass. They appear like pale-coloured insects that are fat and short legged and they move slowly around the surface of the skin. Their eggs appear like white grains of sand attached to the dog's hair. These may be confused with dandruff. Lice are most commonly found around the dog's shoulders, neck, head, ears and anus and cause a great deal of scratching and discomfort for a dog. They do not live for long once off the dog's body and can normally be got rid of by a few good insecticidal baths.

Ticks

Dogs in rural areas often pick up ticks because the tick's natural hosts are sheep and hedgehogs. The tick will live on the ground waiting for a new host to pass by and, once attached to a dog, will feed on the animal's blood. The male tick is often pale in colour and about the size of a match head, while the female, who gorges on the dog's blood, will appear as a deep reddish-black colour and may swell up to the size of a small pea. Ticks are quite easy to spot and as they are slow moving can be easily removed. If they are attached to the animal, however, then great care must be taken not to pull them off and leave the mouth parts buried in the skin as this can cause infections.

A safe method of making the tick release its hold is to apply surgical spirit, alcohol or a strong liquid insect repellent on a cotton bud. Gently move the tick around with the tip of the bud until it comes away. The pest should then be despatched by being crushed between the fingers. Again remember to disinfect the dog's bedding to guard against reinfestation. Bad infestations of ticks should be treated by a strong insecticidal shampoo which can be obtained from the vet.

Worms

Roundworm

Roundworm is the most common worm that infests both dogs and cats. They are yellowish white in colour, resembling spaghetti, pointed at both ends and about 1½–4 inches (4–10cm) in length. Roundworms live in the animal's intestine, producing vast numbers of eggs which are passed in the dog's faeces. The eggs are remarkably tolerant of extremes of temperature and can survive in the open in soil for several years. They are also sticky and can attach themselves to the animal's coat from where they are taken into the body as the animal cleans himself. The fact that so many eggs are produced and that these eggs are able to survive for such long periods out of doors makes it almost impossible for dogs to avoid picking up the infection at some time. Most puppies will be born with roundworm as the mother may have taken in the eggs during the gestation period. These eggs hatch in the gut and become larvae which burrow into the animal's tissue and lie dormant in cysts until hormonal changes in the pregnant mother activate them and they transfer themselves to the unborn puppy. Roundworm eggs can also be passed on by puppies eating their mother's faeces.

The cycle of infection will remain in the kennels until the breeder carries out thorough action on hygiene and worming. Puppies should be wormed against roundworm at about three weeks then six weeks and every six to eight weeks until one year old. After about one year puppies will develop some resistance to roundworm and will then need to be wormed with a dual wormer against tapeworm as well.

Tapeworm

The tapeworm has a number of intermediate hosts which include fleas, lice, rats, mice and other rodents. The most common host is the flea which eats tapeworm eggs. Eggs may sometimes be passed in the excrement of another dog. Having eaten the eggs the flea may attach itself to a dog who then eats the flea when grooming himself, thus the cycle of tapeworm infestation begins.

Tapeworm can also be picked up by your dog eating uncooked meats, dog excrement and raw fish. Often the only indication of a mild infestation of tapeworm is a change in the texture and condition of the dog's coat, and the problem may go unnoticed. A heavy infestation may show itself in a mild diarrhoea with a consequent loss of weight and appetite. An indication of tapeworm is the segments which are passed by the dog in his faeces. These are similar to rice kernels and if alive may be seen to wriggle – they can also sometimes be seen moving around the dog's anus.

The adult tapeworm lives in the intestine of the host dog and fastens itself to the wall of the gut. The worm may grow up to several feet in length and is made up of segments containing packets of eggs.

Worming medication kills the head of the worm and the segments are then passed by the dog and appear like hard dry rice kernels. As a rule an adult dog should be wormed against tapeworm twice a year; once at the start of summer and once again just after the end of summer. Remember that a heavy infestation of fleas can lead to tapeworm.

General Points on Worming

Although it has been previously stated that most puppies are born with roundworm infestation it is also true that this is dependent on the conditions in which they were bred and raised. High standards of hygiene in a breeding establishment can help greatly to reduce the number of puppies born with worms. It is also worth noting that all bitches should be wormed with a dual wormer just before coming into season. Having said this the de-worming of bitches during or before pregnancy cannot guarantee worm-free puppies but will certainly go a long way towards reducing this problem. An appropriate worming preparation can be obtained from your vet.

Hernias

There are various types of hernias that are commonly seen in dogs.

The umbilical hernia is an opening in the wall of the abdomen giving the appearance of a small bulge. Although this can be due to the umbilical cord that leads to the after birth being severed too close to the abdominal wall, most are due to a delayed closure of the umbilical ring. Fortunately, the majority seem to disappear as the puppy grows, and if not, a small operation can be performed on the puppy at a later date to remove it.

A more serious type of hernia is an incarcerated hernia which will also be found on the abdomen. Unlike the soft umbilical hernia that can be easily pushed inwards, the incarcerated hernia will appear as a firm, protruding bulge that cannot be easily pushed inwards. This must be seen by a vet as it can become a danger to the dog.

Another type of hernia is the inguinal hernia where the bulge appears in the groin. This is more common in bitches though a small inguinal can also occur in dogs too. Left to their own devices they may close up but if not then it would be safer to have them repaired. In the case of a bitch this can cause serious problems if she is to be bred from in the future and sometimes this condition is not noticed until she is pregnant.

Pyometra

Pyometra is an abscess that occurs in a bitch's uterus and if it is not removed it can be fatal. This condition tends to be more common in older bitches and is more likely to affect those that have not had a litter of puppies. Pyometra is believed to be caused by a hormonal imbalance, which can occur some time after a bitch comes into season. The bitch may be seen to be acting strangely, drinking large quantities of water and being restless. In certain cases she may be passing large amounts of a thick discharge from her vulva, this discharge having a foul smell and a red or brown colour. This symptom is not always present and other signs must be recognized. A general lack of appetite and no interest in anything may be symptoms of pyometra and she may urinate frequently and may have a high temperature.

Whichever symptoms are showing, if you suspect your bitch of having pyometra it is important to get her to a vet as soon as you can as it is a matter of life and death. The vet will, in most cases, have to remove the bitches uterus in order to save her life.

Patella Luxations

This condition is also referred to as slipping stifle, slipping kneecap or slipping patella.

The problem is the same and is not uncommon in Yorkshire Terriers or any of the other toy breeds of dog. It can be an inherited defect or due to a trauma that the dog suffers. A dog can go through life without ever showing any sign of pain or discomfort and so require no treatment at all. Alternatively a severe condition can cause a dog to be lame in which case a vet will have to perform an operation to help the dog.

Anal Prolapse

The cause of an anal prolapse is a dog's straining very hard to pass a motion. You will find that his bottom around the anus is not clean and all the hair will be stuck together preventing the dog from passing any motion, forcing the lining of the anal passage to protrude. You will find this condition common in a young puppy, as they eat more and pass their motions much more frequently.

You will recognize a partial prolapse by its similarity to haemorrhoids; a raw reddish lump will be seen protruding from the anal area. Should this lump be small then it is possible for you to treat it yourself. The first thing to do is carefully bathe the area with warm water, then using your finger or a thermometer and taking great care using petroleum jelly or cream, gently push the lining back into place. Be extremely careful as this will be a painful time for your dog as the area will be very sore.

Should there be a larger swelling protruding from the dog's anus then this is a much more serious problem as this is a full prolapse which must be urgently treated by a vet.

Anal Scent Glands

On each side of the dog's anus there are small lumps, one each side, which are the anal or scent glands. Dogs will sniff around each other's and the reason for this ritual is to identify one another. Another reason for the glands is that they help the dog to pass his stools. When he does so he will, at the same time, be leaving his mark. This will happen if the dog is on a healthy diet but if the dog's glands get blocked you will find he will drag his bottom along the ground, bite himself around the anus, and you will find hair loss and scabbing. If these anal glands become blocked you will need to release some of the pressure.

The way to do this is to get a towel, hold it over the dog's anus, and then with a couple of fingers apply a little gentle pressure either side of the anus, pressing upwards until a little brown-coloured fluid is released. This takes quite a bit of practice, so if your dog continues to show signs of irritation in this area, ask your vet or a more experienced person to do this for you. If you do not empty the anal glands, your dog could end up with an abscess. If you discover a yellow discharge and the anus is red raw you must take your dog to the vet.

8

International Yorkies

Besides the Yorkshire Terrier's outstanding success in Great Britain, he has become one of the world's most popular dogs and has been particularly sought after as a show dog throughout the world. Early examples arrived on distant shores from the very early days of the breed and, ever since, there has been a demand for breeders to export some of their good stock. Many top British breeders helped with this and their stock has greatly contributed to the breeding programmes in the animals' adopted countries. The export market from the UK

Int. Ch. Ozmilion Justaromance owned by Mrs Bernice Undene.

Author judging in America at the Club Championship Show (1988); the winner was Renie Emmons's Ch. Mistangay Gilbey.

really took off in the 1940s and 1950s with the Yorkshire Terrier becoming the country's top export in the canine world.

The main destination for these exports has been the USA but many have also gone to Europe, South America, Asia and Australia, so that now these humble little dogs from the north of England populate the four corners of the Earth.

America

The history of the Yorkshire Terrier in America begins in the late nineteenth century and not long after the breed was recognized in Britain. The first pair of Yorkshire Terriers to be registered with the American Kennel Club were Butch in 1882 and Daisy in 1884 and both belonged to Mr Andrews of Illinois. The first Yorkshire Terrier to be an American Kennel Club champion of record was Bradford Harry in 1889. He had been imported from England and a descendant of the famous Huddersfield Ben.

Interest in the breed grew and by the turn of the century there were Yorkshire Terrier breeders based in twenty-one of the then forty-five states. Over the early part of the twentieth century interest continued to grow steadily, but it was not until the fourth decade that the breed took off.

In America, Marsha Wolpert with Ch. Wolpert's Lady Fair.

Probably one of the most successful breeders of this time and certainly one of the greatest influences on the American Yorkshire Terrier was Goldie Stone who contributed to the breed's success for over fifty years. Mrs Stone began her Petite kennel in 1929 and went on to produce many great champions over the next five decades. Of these many champions, probably her most famous was Ch. Petite Magnificent Prince who in 1954 became the first US-bred Yorkshire Terrier to win the Best in Show title against all the other breeds.

The 1940s and 1950s saw many high-quality dogs being imported from Britain. These immigrant Yorkshire Terriers were used extensively in breeding as the interest in the breed and the show ring expanded. Importing top English and Irish dogs proved extremely successful for the Wildweir kennel of the famous sisters, Janet Bennett and Joan Gordon. The main basis of their stock came from Harringay, Clu-Mor and Soham lines, with some influence from Buranthea and Johnstounburn. Of these early imports, Ch. Little Sir Model was the most famous as he became the first Yorkshire Terrier to win an All-Breed Best in Show title at an American show. This was the beginning of the sisters' success that has since dominated York-

In America, Fred Wolpert with Ch. Wolpert's Mighty Jack.

shire Terriers in America. Although their imported dogs were very successful in the show arena, they provided even more success with their breeding and produced many champions and quality stock for the kennel. This has led to the Wildweir kennel producing more American champions than any other kennel and a vast number of records and wins along the way. One such record is that held by their home-bred Ch. Wildweir Pomp 'n' Circumstance who, as a stud-dog sired ninety-five champions making him the most influential Yorkshire Terrier stud-dog in America.

The 1960s saw the formation of the Mayfair Kennels by Ann Seranne, who became and has remained a major influence on the breed. In 1962, she purchased Am. and Can. Ch. Topsy of Tolestar as a foundation bitch who went on to produce some excellent stock and a number of champions for her owner. In 1966 Anne Seranne was joined by Barbara Wolferman and this dynamic partnership has been successful ever since with well over fifty champions attributable to their Mayfair-Barban kennel. Probably their most famous dog was their top-winning Am. and Can. Ch. Gaytonglen Teddy of Mayfair.

Initially combining the Mayfair-Barban breeding with his own Ch. Frojo's Blue Buttons of Maybelle, Fred Wolpert and Marsha have

179

From left to right: Kathleen Kolbert's Am. Ch. Ozmilion Playboy, his daughter Ch. Windsor Gayelyn Gilded Lily and Ch. Gayelyn Gilded Lily.

Linda and Eddy Nicholson's very famous Am. Ch. Nikko's Rolls Royce Corniche, bred by Mr and Mrs Lipman.

Barbra and Bill Switzer's top-winning Am. and Can. Ch. Ce De Higgens, shown by their daughter Marlene, winning Best in Show at Westminster. Judge, Mrs Anne Roger Clark.

produced a steady string of champions from the late 1960s to the present day. They further strengthened their Wolpert kennel based in Philadelphia with top-quality stock imported from Britain during the mid-1980s and have continued to be very successful.

Another successful partnership has been that of the Windsor-Gayelyn kennel. Both owners Kathleen Kolbert and Marilyn Koenig had been successful with their own kennels before uniting in 1969. They have had a succession of champions ever since and their strong breeding programmes were further strengthened with the addition of Ch. Ozmilion Playboy in 1972.

Based in New Hampshire is the On Top of the Line kennel, owned by Linda and Ed Nicholson. They owned the famous Am. Ch. Nikkos Rolls Royce Corniche who was bred by Mr and Mrs Lipman.

Probably the most famous Yorkshire Terrier in the breed's history in America must be Am. and Can. Ch. Ce De Higgens. In 1978 he won the Best in Show award at the Westminster Show under the famous judge Anne Rogers-Clark. He was bred and owned by Barbara and Bill Switzer and was shown by their daughter Marlene.

Madame Jaufrit Sylvette's Fr. Ch. Tiffany de l'Eclipse Royale.

Europe

In France, in the heart of Paris, Madam Duchatel did much to popularize the Yorkshire Terrier in Europe while dominating for nearly thirty years the *Club Français Du Terrier Du Yorkshire*; she was the secretary of the club and later became president. All her original Yorkshire Terriers were Hampark stock from Bill Wilkinson in England and these were supplemented in the early 1970s when Ozmilion stock was added.

Also in France, Madame Mona Jammas of the Lucky Lad kennel started her breeding with stock from the Plantation Hall and Ozmilion lines. Her most famous winner was Rocky Lucky Lad who was a son of Fr. and Bel. Ch. Ozmilion Inclination. Another notable French breeder is Madame Jaufrit Sylvette, who has been devoted to her De L'Eclipse Royale Yorkshire Terriers; her most famous top-winning bitch was Int. Ch. Tiffany De L'Eclipse Royale.

Mark Mansuet with his famous De Monderlay dogs has also achieved much success – his stock is mainly from the Ozmilion and Blairsville lines. His first international champion was Int. Ch. Ozmilion True Romance; he also bred the very famous Ch. Royal Flash De Monderlay, who was a top winner at a World Championship Show. Another breeding success was his export to Britain, Ch. Bananas Du Domaine De Monderlay At Gaysteps, who was campaigned in Britain by Mrs A. Fisher.

In recent years, Ronny and Maria Englen have had much success from their kennel at Antwerp in Belgium. They started their kennel in 1967 with both Invincia and Johnstounburn stock, which they purchased directly from Scotland. This has led to a string of champions for their Millmore and My Precious kennels; probably, their most famous champion is Ch. Ever Trouble of Millmore.

Yorkshire Terriers have become very popular in Germany with a number of notable kennels. Among these are Jurgen Grun and Armin Kriechbaumer with their famous Bloomsbury Yorkshire Terriers, including their top-winning bitch Bloomsbury Happiness Love. Another successful West German kennel has been the Armani kennel of Armand Klein, who founded his kennel on Ozmilion stock and has bred many good champions including the well-known winner Ch. Armani's Mr Just Me.

In Belgium, Mr and Mrs Ronny Engelen's famous Ch. Ever Trouble of Millmore.

183

In Germany, Jurgen Grun's top-winning bitch, Ch. Bloomsbury Happiness Love.

In Sweden in early 1970 Henrick Johansson started his Henrickville kennel with the Carlwyn and Ozmilion lines. At a later date he added the Deebees line to his breeding programme and has bred many fine dogs. Working side by side in Sweden has been Bernice Undene who also started her Debonaire kennel in the early 1970s where she has

In Germany, Armand Klien's famous Ch. Armanis Mr Just Me.

In Sweden, Bernice Undene's Swed., Fin. and Nor. Ch.
Debonaire's High-Muck-A-Muck.

become the top producer and breeder of Yorkshire Terriers. She
started with mainly Ozmilion stock and then added Carmady stock.
Much later she introduced Parcvern stock to her kennel, which has
continued to be successful. Amongst her well-known dogs is Swed.
Fin. and Nor. Ch. Debonaires High Muck-A-Muck. Meanwhile in
Finland, Elizabeth Dahlquish has bred and shown many excellent
dogs from her Acaockwills kennel; probably her best-known champion is Ch. Acaockwills Barbie Bee.

Italy is the home of many excellent Yorkshire Terriers bred by
Antonella Tomaselli at her Antiche Mura kennel. Probably her two
most famous winners were Ch. Agapi Delle Antiche Mura and Chif-
fonette, who was sired by Bel. Ch. Flamboyant. Also in Italy, Mrs
Sonia Pagani has been very hard working on the breed; starting out
with Beechrise, Meadpark and Ozmilion lines she later introduced
the Millmoor lines and has produced many excellent dogs.

9

Best in Show Winners

At this stage I would like to pay tribute to the famous Yorkshire Terriers who have hit the headlines over the years by becoming Supreme Best in Show winners at the All-Breed Championship Shows.

The first one was Mrs Renton's Ch. Pagnell Prima Donna of Wiske bred by Mrs Groom; this was followed by her brother, Ch. Pagnell Peter Pan who was owned and bred by Mrs Groom. Next was Mrs Mary Haye's home-bred Ch. Chantmarles Snuff Box. The line follows with Mrs D. Beech's Ch. Deebees Beebee bred by Mrs C.M. Pitcher, and Mr and Mrs Lister's home-bred Ch. Blairsville Most Royal, and to succeed him, home-bred Ch. Blairsville Royal Seal. Next to achieve this honour was Ch. Wykebank Tinkerbell, belonging to Mr and Mrs A. Blamires. Finally, our own Ch. Ozmilion Hopelessly In Love, then Ch. Ozmilion Dedication followed by his son, Ch. and Ir. Ch. Ozmilion Sensation. I have included all their pedigrees for reference (*see* pages 189–98).

All of the above champions have done a great deal to promote the popularity of this breed over the years but one must remember that to achieve this high accolade takes a great deal of work and dedication.

Record-Holders in the Breed

The top-winning dog of all time is the author's Ch. Ozmilion Dedication with a total of 52 CCs.

Top-winning bitch is Mrs V. Sameja Hilliard's Ch. Verolian Temptress with Ozmilion with a total of 39 CCs.

Ch. Ozmilion Jubilation was top sire for 1974, 1975, 1982, 1983, 1984, 1985 and 1986, and sired fourteen British champions.

Ch. Ozmilion Heart's Desire is dam to five British champions.

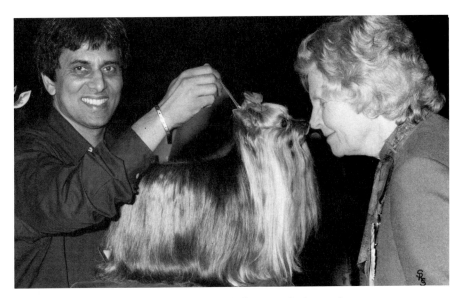

The author's top-winning Yorkshire Terrier of all time and winner of
52 CCs, Ch. Ozmilion Dedication kissing the famous all-rounder
judge Nora Down after winning Best in Show at the United
Kingdom Toy Dog Championship Show.

Veronica Sameja-Hilliard
with her top CC-winning
bitch, Ch. Verolian
Temptress with Ozmilion,
winner of 39 CCs.

Ch. and Ir. Ch. Ozmilion Jubilation Top Sire in the breed and a sire to 14 British champions; Top Sire 1974, 1975, 1982, 1983, 1984, 1985 and 1986.

Ch. Ozmilion Hearts Desire, Top Brood-Bitch, dam to 5 British champions.

Best in Show Winners Pedigrees

Mrs K. Renton's Ch. Pagnell Prima Donna of Wiske, winner of Best in Show, All-Breed Championship Show.

PEDIGREE		
NAME Ch. Pagnell Prima Donna of Wiske **SEX** Bitch **BORN** 1 May 1957 **OWNER** Mrs K. Renton **BREEDER** Mrs S.I. Groom		
PARENTS	**GRANDPARENTS**	**GREAT GRANDPARENTS**
SIRE Ch. Burgwallis Little Nip	**SIRE** Burgwallis Waggie	**SIRE** Ch. Splendour of Invincia
		DAM Powder Puff
	DAM Stanhope Queen	**SIRE** Blue Ink
		DAM Sunflower
DAM Prisim of Johnstounburn	**SIRE** Ch. & Ir. Ch. Mr Pim of Johnstounburn	**SIRE** Parkview Prince
		DAM Flea of Johnstounburn
	DAM Lady of the Lake	**SIRE** Little Tommy Tucker
		DAM Patite Patsey

Mrs S.I. Groom's Ch. Pagnell Peter Pan, winner of Best in Show, All-Breed Championship Show.

PEDIGREE		
NAME Ch. Pagnell Peter Pan **SEX** Dog **BORN** 17 October 1961 **OWNER/BREEDER** Mrs S.I. Groom		
PARENTS	**GRANDPARENTS**	**GREAT GRANDPARENTS**
SIRE Ch. Burgwallis Little Nip	**SIRE** Burgwallis Little Nip	**SIRE** Ch. Splendour of Invincia
		DAM Powder Puff
	DAM Stanhope Queen	**SIRE** Blue Ink
		DAM Sunflower
DAM Prisim of Johnstounburn	**SIRE** Ch. & Ir. Ch. Mr Pim of Johnstounburn	**SIRE** Parkview Prince
		DAM Flea of Johnstounburn
	DAM Lady of the Lake	**SIRE** Little Tommy Tucker
		DAM Patite Patsey

Mary Hayes' Ch. Chantmarles Snuff Box, winner of Best in Show, All-Breed Championship Show.

PEDIGREE		
NAME Ch. Chantmarles Snuff Box **SEX** Bitch **BORN** 31 October 1968 **OWNER/BREEDER** Mrs Mary Hayes		
PARENTS	**GRANDPARENTS**	**GREAT GRANDPARENTS**
SIRE Macstroud's Whitecross Dandini	**SIRE** Wyhylda Tiny Tim	**SIRE** Wyhylda Tim the Swanker
		DAM Wyhylda Toots
	DAM Whitecross Jennie	**SIRE** Whitecross Boy Blue
		DAM Whitecross Mendip Girl
DAM Mycariad Stargazer	**SIRE** Bright Star of Yarnum	**SIRE** Ch. Elmslade Galahad of Yadnum
		DAM Golden Ember of Yadnum
	DAM Hempseed Diamondlil	**SIRE** Yorkfold Grand Pim
		DAM Hempseed Queen Bee

Mr D. Beech's Ch. Deebees Bee Bee, winner of Best in Show, All-Breed Championship Show.

PEDIGREE		
NAME Ch. Deebees Beebee **SEX** Bitch **BORN** 11 September 1969 **OWNER** Mrs D. Beech **BREEDER** Mrs C.M. Pitcher		
PARENTS	**GRANDPARENTS**	**GREAT GRANDPARENTS**
SIRE Deebees Bumble Boy	**SIRE** Deebees Tommy Tucker	**SIRE** Deebees Goodiff Cracker
		DAM Deebees Caramia
	DAM Deebees Golden Penny	**SIRE** Deebees Golden Plume
		DAM Ch. Deebees Little Dodo
DAM Wee Polly Fisher of Whipton	**SIRE** Tosh of Hillhead	**SIRE** Tansleydale Special
		DAM Sally of Tansleydale
	DAM Kitty of Sparry	**SIRE** Raventon Rascal
		DAM Gay of Sparry

Mr and Mrs B. Lister's Ch. Blairsville Most Royale, Best in Show, All-Breed Championship Show.

PEDIGREE		
NAME Ch. Blairsville Most Royale **SEX** Bitch **BORN** 12 May 1971 **OWNER/BREEDER** Mr & Mrs B. Lister		
PARENTS	**GRANDPARENTS**	**GREAT GRANDPARENTS**
SIRE Ch. Whisperdales Temujin	**SIRE** Ravelin Little Jimmy	**SIRE** Dusty Jimmy of Aspenden
		DAM Chingford Sweet Sue
	DAM Ch. Whisperdales Phirno Carmen	**SIRE** Champion Ravelin Gaiety Boy
		DAM Blue Biddy
DAM Ch. Blairsville Shirene	**SIRE** Ch. Blairsville Boy Wonder	**SIRE** Leodian Smart Boy
		DAM Blairsville Lady
	DAM Blairsville Belinda	**SIRE** Ch. Burgwallis Vikki
		DAM Leodian Kandy Katy

Mr and Mrs B. Lister's famous Ch. Blairsville Royal Seal, winner of Best in Show at All-Breed Championship Show.

PEDIGREE		
NAME Ch. Blairsville Royal Seal **SEX** Dog **BORN** 2 May 1974 **OWNER/BREEDER** Mr & Mrs B. Lister		
PARENTS	**GRANDPARENTS**	**GREAT GRANDPARENTS**
SIRE Ch. Beechrise Surprise	**SIRE** Ch. Beechrise Superb	**SIRE** Ch. Pagnell Peter Pan
		DAM Beechrise Pixie
	DAM Jane Cutler	**SIRE** Sorreldene Shadow
		DAM Amber Socks
DAM Ch. Blairsville Most Royal	**SIRE** Ch. Whisperdales Temujin	**SIRE** Ravelin Little Jimmy
		DAM Ch. Whisperdales Phirno Carmen
	DAM Ch. Blairsville Shirene	**SIRE** Ch. Blairsville Boy Wonder
		DAM Blairsville Belinda

Joyce Blamire with her most famous Ch. Wykebank Tinkerbell, winner of Best in Show, All-Breed Championship Show.

PEDIGREE		
NAME Ch. Wykebank Tinkerbell **SEX** Bitch **BORN** 24 February 1978 **OWNER/BREEDER** Mr A. Blamires		
PARENTS	**GRANDPARENTS**	**GREAT GRANDPARENTS**
SIRE Blairsville Royal Monarch	**SIRE** Ch. & Ir. Ch. Ozmilion Jubilation	**SIRE** Ch. Ozmilion My Imagination
		DAM Ozmilion Justine
	DAM Ch. Blairsville Most Royal	**SIRE** Ch. Whisperdale Tamujin
		DAM Ch. Blairsville Shirene
DAM Wykebank Vanity Fair	**SIRE** Ch. & Ir. Ch. Ozmilion Jubilation	**SIRE** Ch. Ozmilion My Imagination
		DAM Ozmilion Justine
	DAM Ch. Wykebank Impeccable	**SIRE** Beechrise Splendid
		DAM Wykebank Debutante

The author's Ch. Ozmilion Hopelessly In Love, winner of Best in Show at All-Breed Championship Show.

PEDIGREE		
NAME Ch. Ozmilion Hopelessly in Love **SEX** Bitch **BORN** 6 July 1983 **BREEDER** Mr Osman A. Sameja		
PARENTS	**GRANDPARENTS**	**GREAT GRANDPARENTS**
SIRE Ch. Ozmilion Distinction	**SIRE** Ch. & Ir. Ch. Ozmilion Jubilation	**SIRE** Ch. Ozmilion My Imagination
		DAM Ozmilion Justine
	DAM Ozmilion Summer Illusion	**SIRE** Ch. Heavenly Blue of Wiske
		DAM Blue Gem of Highfield
DAM Ch. Ozmilion Flames of Desire	**SIRE** Ch. & Ir. Ch. Ozmilion Jubilation	**SIRE** Ch. Ozmilion My Imagination
		DAM Ozmilion Justine
	DAM Ch. Ozmilion Exageration	**SIRE** Ch. Ozmilion My Imagination
		DAM Ch. & Ir. Ch. Ozmilion Modesty

The author's Ch. Ozmilion Dedication, winner of Best in Show at All-Breed Championship Show.

PEDIGREE		
NAME Ch. Ozmilion Dedication **SEX** Dog **BORN** 20 April 1985 **OWNER/BREEDER** Mr Osman A. Sameja		
PARENTS	**GRANDPARENTS**	**GREAT GRANDPARENTS**
SIRE Ch. Ozmilion Admiration	**SIRE** Ch. Ozmilion Invitation	**SIRE** Ch. Ozmilion Expectation
		DAM Ch. Ozmilion Exageration
	DAM Ch. Ozmilion Love Romance	**SIRE** Ch. Ozmilion Tradition
		DAM Ch. Ozmilion Heart's Desire
DAM Ch. Ozmilion Heart's Desire	**SIRE** Ch. Ozmilion Premonition	**SIRE** Ch. Ozmilion Distinction
		DAM Ch. Ozmilion Just Imagine
	DAM Int. Ch. Ozmilion Justaromance	**SIRE** Ch. My Precious Joss
		DAM Ch. Ozmilion Just Imagine

The author's Ch. and Ir. Ch. Ozmilion Sensation, winner of Best in Show at All-Breed Championship Show.

PEDIGREE		
NAME Ch. & Ir. Ch. Ozmilion Sensation **SEX** Dog **BORN** 10 August 1986 **OWNER/BREEDER** Mr Osman A. Sameja		
PARENTS	**GRANDPARENTS**	**GREAT GRANDPARENTS**
SIRE Ch. Ozmilion Dedication	**SIRE** Ch. Ozmilion Admiration	**SIRE** Ch. Ozmilion Invitation
		DAM Ch. Ozmilion Love Romance
	DAM Ch. Ozmilion Heart's Desire	**SIRE** Ch. Ozmilion Premonition
		DAM Int. Ch. Ozmilion Just A Romance
DAM Ch. Ozmilion Love Romance	**SIRE** Ch. Ozmilion Tradition	**SIRE** Ch. Ozmilion Premonition
		DAM Ch. Ozmilion Exageration
	DAM Ch. Ozmilion Heart's Desire	**SIRE** Ch. Ozmilion Premonition
		DAM Int. Ch. Ozmilion Justaromance

Best Yorkshire Terrier Champions 1947–1990

Name of Champion	Sex	Sire	Dam	Breeder	Owner	Date of Birth
1947						
Bens Blue Pride	D	Blue Flash	Jill	Mr Roper	Mr Williamson	8.7.44
Lady Nada	B	Wee Willie Winkie	Little Flower	Mrs R. Allen	Mrs Hebson	9.9.42
1948						
Hebsonian Jealousy	B	Gay Prince	Hebsonian Harana	Mrs Hebson	Mrs Hebson	10.3.49
Weeplustoo of Achmonie	B	Sweet Memory of Achmonie	Isolda of Achmonie	Miss Macdonald	Miss Macdonald	9.5.45
Starlight	D	Marten Teddy	Adora	Mr Orford	Mrs Hargreaves	15.10.45
1949						
Wee Don of Atherleigh	D	Don Progresso	Beauty of Atherleigh	Mr Hayes	Mr Hayes	13.9.45
McCay of Achmonie	D	Nigella	Sophie of Achmonie	Miss Macdonald	Miss Macdonald	21.4.46
Splendour of Invincia	D	Invincia Masher	Olie of Invincia	Mrs Swan	Mrs Swan	16.7.47
Vemair Parkview Preview	D	Parkview Prince	Parkview Dinky	Mr Bain	Mrs Mair	12.5.46
Tufty of Johnstounburn	B	Midge's Pal	Hazy of Johnstounburn	Mrs Crookshank	Mrs Crookshank	3.5.45
1950						
Blue Dolly	B	Ch. Bens Blue Pride	Little Marionette	Mr Coates	Mr Coates	2.4.46
Mr Pim of Johnstounburn	D	Parkview Prince	Flea of Johnstounburn	Mr Sturrock	Mrs Crookshank	29.2.47
Dinah Beau	B	Bridle Copper King	Beauty of Atherleigh	Mr Hayes	Miss Hartley	24.6.48
Winpal Arine	B	Soham Caryle	Anita of Soham	Lady E. Windham-Dawson	Miss Palmer	13.2.47
1951						
Wee Gertrude	B	Monican Punch	Queenie's Pride	Mr Thurlow	Mrs Chard & Miss Fairchild	16.1.48

Name of Champion	Sex	Sire	Dam	Breeder	Owner	Date of Birth
Feona of Phylreyne	B	Christoeferobin of Phylreyne	Phylreyne Irrepressible	Mrs Raine	Mrs Raine	12.2.48
Vemair Principal Boy	D	Parkview Prince	Frosty of Johnstounburn	Mr Bain	Mrs Mair	28.6.49
Sorreldene Honey Son of the Vale	D	Harringay Little Dandy	Pretty Paulette	Mrs Sharp	Mrs Bradley	25.11.48
Hopwood Camelia	B	Invincia Masher	Invincia Margretta	Mrs Swan	Miss Martin	9.3.48
Wee Blue Atom	D	Little Boy Blue	Our Sue	Mrs E. Latliff	Mrs Overet	20.7.48
Martynwyns Golden Girl	B	Martin Teddy	Marian Martinette	Mr Coates	Mrs Montgomery	24.4.48
Martynwyns Surprise of Atherleigh	D	Invincia Masher	Pat of Atherleigh	Mr Hayes	Mr Coates	24.11.47
1952						
Adora of Invincia	B	Invincia Masher	Olie of Invincia	Mrs Swan	Mrs Swan	5.6.48
Tatiania of Invincia	B	Pride of Invincia	Nancy of Invincia	Mrs Swan	Mrs Stirk	25.9.48
Sunstar of Invincia	B	Invincia Masher	Margie of Invincia	Mrs Swan	Mrs Swan	5.6.50
Blue Belle	B	Wee Blue Atom	Blue Bonnet	Miss Noakes	Miss Noakes	21.8.50
Someone of Achmonie	D	Ch. McCay of Achmonie	Feona of Achmonie	Miss Macdonald	Miss Macdonald	–
Wee Eve of Yadnum	B	Int. Ch. Mr Pim of Johnstounburn	Scotford Queen	Mr Scott	Mrs Munday	10.8.51
Kelsbro Quality Boy	D	Gayways Little Trotters	Dinkie Blue	Mrs Cross	Mrs Cross	28.6.49
Firhill Fairy	B	Midge's Pal	Miss Monty	Mr Anderson	Mrs Pannett	30.9.48
Winpal Henrietta	B	Henry of Soham	Prunella of Achmonie	Miss Macdonald	Miss Palmer	30.3.49
Jacaranda Beauty	B	Little Boy Blue	Bridle Sweetbrier	Mrs Montgomery	Mrs Montgomery	25.1.51
1953						
Vemair Spider	D	Midge's Pal	Cogee Dinah	Mr Johnson	Mrs Mair	30.9.48
Martynwyns Debonaire	D	Little Boy Blue	Our Sue	Mrs Latliff	Mr Coates	4.10.49
Medium of Johnstounburn	B	Midge's Pal	Misty of Johnstounburn	Mrs Crookshank	Mrs Crookshank	23.10.50

Name of Champion	Sex	Sire	Dam	Breeder	Owner	Date of Birth
Aerial of Winpal	B	Prince Cosmo of Winpal	Ch. Winpal Arine	Miss Palmer	Miss Palmer	4.7.52
Eoforwic Envoy of Yadnum	D	Blue Guinea of Yadnum	Florentina of Yadnum	Mrs Prosser	Mrs Munday	1.7.50
Jessica of Westridge	B	Ch. Martynwyns Surprise of Atherleigh	Pauline of Westridge	Mr Grist	Mr Grist	19.7.51
Stirkean Chota Sahib	D	Splendour of Invincia	Empress of Invincia	Mrs Swan	Mrs Stirk	22.8.51
Butibel Perseus	D	Bawdigan Prince Charming	Lovely Blue Prince	Mrs Russell	Mrs Russell	20.11.49
1954						
Midnight Gold of Yadnum	D	Pip the Piper	Lady Prudence of Yadnum	Mrs Donaldson	Mrs Munday	29.4.53
Myrtle of Johnstounburn	B	Int. Ch. Mr Pim of Johnstounburn	Misty of Johnstounburn	Mrs Crookshank	Mrs Crookshank	8.7.49
Faye of Phylreyne	B	Sorreldene Honeyson of The Vale	Fiona of Phylreyne	Mrs Raine	Mrs Raine	10.4.52
1955						
Burgwallis Little Nip	D	Burgwallis Waggie	Stanhope Queen	Mr Howard	Mrs Betton	29.6.52
Sehow Independent	B	Pagham Sehow Special	Pennywort of Pagham	Miss Marter	Miss Howes	18.5.53
Wadeholme Little Mitzi	B	Peddler Boy	Sehow Hopeful	Mrs Drake	Mrs Wade	19.12.52
Stirkean Kandy Boy	D	Ch. Stirkean Chota Sahib	Trix of Invincia	Mrs Stirk	Mrs Stirk	23.12.53
Martynwyns Adora	B	Martynwyns Teddy	Wee Suzetta	Mrs Latliff	Mrs Seymour	25.1.53
Epperstone Bon Ton	D	Epperstone Surprise	Mam's Little Pal	Mrs Read	Mrs Hill	5.6.53
Vemair Uncle Sam	D	Ch. Vemair Principal Boy	Memorosa Jill	Mr Hall	Mrs Mair	4.7.52
Eastgrove Gay Boy	D	Gayway Little Trotters	Susan's Wee Lady	Mr Ford	Mrs Hargreaves	14.1.52
Delia Erlcour	B	Victory Boy	Miretta Marianne	Mrs Batsford	Mrs Batsford	10.6.53
Blue Symon	D	Golden Fame	Dinah is Good	Miss Armstrong	Mrs John	29.9.51

Name of Champion	Sex	Sire	Dam	Breeder	Owner	Date of Birth
1956						
Pipit of Johnstounburn	B	Int. Ch. Mr Pim of Johnstounburn	Pixy of Johnstounburn	Mrs Crookshank	Mrs Crookshank	6.9.54
Burantheas Angel Bright	B	Int. Ch. Mr Pim of Johnstounburn	Burantheas Paris Jewel	M. Burfield	M. Burfield	29.4.54
Hilaire of Pookshill	D	Starlight of Pookshill	Rosalinda of Erlcour	Mrs Batsford	Mrs Wood	23.1.54
Moon Glow of Yadnum	D	Sir Gay of Yadnum	Pretty Paulette	Mrs Sharpe	Mrs Sharpe	13.6.55
Aureola of Winpal	B	Butibel Mercury	Aimee of Winpal	Miss Palmer	Miss Palmer	24.10.52
1957						
Cressida of Erlcour	B	Dandini of Erlcour	Miretta Marianne	Mrs Batsford	Mrs Batsford	22.4.56
Martini	D	Ch. Splendour of Invincia	Cherie of Invincia	Mrs Swan	Mrs Beech	1.8.53
Blue Orchid of Hilfore	B	Totis Treasure	Midget of Hilfore	Mrs Seymour	Mrs Seymour	8.8.55
Prim of Johnstounburn	B	Int. Ch. Mr Pim of Johnstounburn	Lady of the Lake	Mr Brown	D. Rossitar	25.7.55
Pimbron of Johnstounburn	D	Int. Ch. Mr Pim of Johnstounburn	Lady of the Lake	Mr Brown	Mr M.D.Y. Lowrie	4.7.54
Symons Querida of Tolestar	B	Ch. Blue Symon	Honey Queen	Mrs John	Mrs Tole	19.9.54
1958						
Bystander's Replica	D	The Young Aristocrat	Jill	Miss S. Logan	Miss S. Logan	22.8.54
Coulgorm Chloe	B	Coulgorm Remus	Versatile Veronica	Mr A. Hughs	Mrs C. Hutchin	10.5.56
Deebees Stirkeans Faustina	B	Ch. Stirkeans Chota Sahib	Stirkeans Astolat Enchantress	Mrs E.A. Stirk	Mrs S.D. Beech	15.2.57
June's Boy	D	Little Boy Blue	Dainty Princess Suzanne	Mrs E. Latliff	Mr J. Latliff	19.10.53
Ravelin Gaiety Boy	D	Ravelin Golden Boy	Changford Sweet Sue	Mrs E. Latliff	Miss P.I. Noakes	13.10.55
Sir Lancelot of Astolat	D	Pagham Sehow Special	Astolat Nicolette	Mrs Charlton-Haw	Mrs Charlton-Haw	6.2.56
Societyraw Dog Friday	D	Fawn of Fiskerton	Lassie of Societyraw	Mrs J. Barrs	Mr & Mrs E. Barrs	27.4.56
Stirkeans Rhapsody	D	Ch. Stirkeans Chota Sahib	Stirkeans Anne Marie of Winpal	Mrs E. Stirk	Mrs E. Stirk	21.2.57

Name of Champion	Sex	Sire	Dam	Breeder	Owner	Date of Birth
1959						
Buranthea's Doutelle	D	Int. Ch. Mr Pim of Johnstounburn	Buranthea's York Sensation	M. Burfield	M. Burfield	8.5.57
Don Carlos of Progresso	D	Ch. Martynwyns Wee Teddy	Shirlorn Sally	Mrs C. Hutchin	Mrs C. Hutchin	20.12.57
Elaine of Astolat	B	Pagham Sehow Special	Astolat Nicolette	Mrs Charlton-Haw	Mrs Charlton-Haw	6.2.56
Pagnell Prima Donna of Wiske	B	Ch. Burgwallis Little Nip	Prism of Johnstounburn	Mrs S.I. Groom	Mrs K.M. Renton	1.5.57
Pedimins Piper	D	Bonclad of Invincia	Pedimins Parade	Mr G. Porter	Mr G. Porter	22.10.57
Stirkeans Astonoff Horatio	D	Stirkeans Teekhai	Astonoff Victory Victorias	Mrs Etherington	Mrs E. Stirk	31.3.58
1960						
Deebees Campari	D	Ch. Stirkeans Chota Sahib	Deebees Lillet	Mrs S.D. Beech	Mrs S.D. Beech	1.5.59
Burgwallis Vikki	D	Ch. Burgwallis Little Nip	Prism of Johnstounburn	Mrs S.I. Groom	Mrs M. Betton	1.5.57
Hampark Dandy	D	Ear-Wi-Go of Tzumiao	Chota Memsahib	Mr R. Wilkinson	Mr W. Wilkinson	26.6.58
My Sweet Susanne	B	Totis Treasure	Gloria's Girl	Mrs D.R. Baynes	Mrs D.R. Baynes	24.6.58
Sungold Supreme	B	Happy Warrior of Saughey	Tauntsom Polly Anna	Mr D.A. Smith	Mr D.A. Smith	22.5.58
Wadeholme Happy Quest	D	Wadeholme Staraza of Clu-Mor	Wadeholme Merry Maid	Mrs L.J. Wade	Mrs L.J. Wade	12.7.57
1961						
Adora Junior of Hilfore	B	Ravelin Golden Boy	Ch. Martynwyns Adora	Mrs V. Seymour	Mr H.T. Seymour	30.7.58
Burgwallis Brideen	B	Ch. Burgwallis Little Nip	Little Sheba	Mrs A. Brown	Mrs M. Betton	15.2.58
Deebees Isa La Bella	B	Ch. Stirkeans Chota Sahib	Deebees Lillet	Mrs S.D. Beech	Mrs S.D. Beech	1.5.59

203

Name of Champion	Sex	Sire	Dam	Breeder	Owner	Date of Birth
Doone of Wiske	B	Burgwallis Sukyboy	Madcap Molly	Mr W. Quin	Mrs K. Renton	12.3.59
Fuchsia of Fiskerton	B	Fiskerton Limelight of Lilactime	Stirkeans Frisky Dot	Mrs V. Moyes	Mrs V. Moyes	26.3.58
Glamour Boy of Glengonner	D	Little Tot of Glengonner	Queen of Birkburn	Mr A. Bennie	Mr D.A. Peck	11.6.59
Leyham Mascot	D	Ch. June's Boy	Kim's Starlight	Mrs D. Mayall	Mrs D. Mayall	31.12.58
Mamma's Little Topper	D	Beechrise Dandy	Halloween of Grenbar	Mr J. Walker	Mrs K. Cherryholme	20.7.58
Progress of Progresso	D	Int. Ch. Don Carlos of Progresso	Ch. Coulgorm Chloe	Mrs C. Hutchin	Mrs C. Hutchin	2.4.59
Stirkeans Puff Puffin	B	Ch. Stirkeans Chota Sahib	Stirkeans Astolat Enchantress	Mrs E.A. Stirk	Mrs E.A. Stirk	18.5.58
1962						
Deebees Hot Toddy	D	Ch. Deebees Campari	Deebees Phoebe	Mrs S.D. Beech	Mrs S.D. Beech	9.6.60
Elmsglade Galahad of Yadnum	D	Elmsglade Chuffty	Elmsglade Moon Maiden	Mrs M. Slade	Mrs E. Munday	11.8.60
Guytons Spring Blossom	B	Bonnies Apple Blossom	Our Pepita	Mr G. Kniveton	Mr G. Kniveton	17.5.60
Jacaranda Blue Mischief	B	Jacaranda Jolly Boy	Jacaranda Petite	Mrs J. Montgomery	Mrs J. Montgomery	1.2.61
Kelsbro Blue Pete	D	Kelsbro Brigadier	Kelsbro Pretty Peggy	Mr H. Cross	Mr H. Cross	6.11.59
Melody Maker of Embyll	B	Int. Ch. Don Carlos of Progresso	Little Blue Wonder	Mr W.E. Everett	Mrs C. Hutchin	11.12.59
Pontana Prodigy Dainty	B	Pedimins Prodigy	Tulip Design	Mrs G. Howells	Mrs G. Howells	9.12.60
Stirkeans Mr Tim	D	Stirkeans Titmouse	Stirkeans Krakawin	Mrs E. Stirk	Mrs E. Stirk	13.5.60
Sundance of Wiske	B	Ch. Burgwallis Vikki	Vanessa of Wiske	Mrs K.M. Renton	Mrs K.M. Renton	18.8.59
1963						
Charm of Wadeholme	B	Wadeholme Staraza of Clu-Mor	Wadeholme Wee Rebel	Mrs L.J. Wade	Mrs L.J. Wade	7.10.59
Deebees Caromia	B	Ch. Deebees Hot Toddy	Deebees Invincia Rosemary	Mrs D. Beech	Mrs D. Beech	7.11.61

Name of Champion	Sex	Sire	Dam	Breeder	Owner	Date of Birth
Hopwood Desirable	D	Hopwood Torville Majestic	Hopwood Fantasia	Miss E. Martin	Mr J.W. Hutchinson	8.3.59
Pagnell Peter Pan	D	Ch. Burgwallis Little Nip	Prism of Johnstounburn	Mrs S.I. Groom	Mrs S.I. Groom	17.10.61
Tzumiao's Cheetah of Martinez	B	Ear-Wi-Go of Tzumiao	Victoria's Pride	Mr & Mrs Martin	E. Gilbert	25.5.60
Wencoes Wendolene	B	Ear-Wi-Go of Tzumiao	Pedimins Proposal	Miss W. Schofield	Miss W. Schofield	25.6.61
Yorkfold Wrupert Bear	D	Yorkfold Chocolate Boy	Yorkfold Koala	Mrs Rossitar	Mrs Rossitar	6.9.61
1964						
Burantheas Saint Malachy	D	Piccolo Patrico	Burantheas Boutelle Replica	M. Burfield	M. Burfield	25.11.60
Deebees Little Dodo	B	Deebees Stirkeans Drummer Boy	Deebees Prunella of Invincia	Mrs D. Beech	Mrs D. Beech	11.2.62
Goodiff Blue Dragon	D	Ch. Hampark Dandy	Trixie of Winpal	Mr M.G. Taylor	Mr G. Crowther	6.10.61
Millfield Mandy	B	Pagnell Brigadier	Solandra Blue Binky	Mrs C. Bailey	Mrs M. Hepworth	9.3.62
Minvera of Johnstounburn	B	Ch. Primbron of Johnstounburn	Muffit of Johnstounburn	Mrs Crookshank	Mrs M.D. Lowrie	9.10.61
Phirno Magic Moment	B	Ch. Ravelin Gaiety Boy	Phirno Miss Mandy	Miss P. Noakes	Miss P. Noakes	12.9.62
Progresso Lover Boy	D	Ch. Progress of Progresso	Pink Girl of Progresso	Mrs C. Hutchin	Mrs C. Hutchin	14.1.62
Romance of Wiske	B	Templevale of Pertinacious	Miss Bessie Bon	Mrs J.R. Milnes	Mrs K.M. Renton	2.10.62
Skyrona Blue Prince	D	Baby Peachy of Rosehara	Woldsdene Blue Rose	Mrs G. Sykes	Mrs G. Sykes	15.7.62
Yorkfold McPickle	D	Ch. Burantheas Saint Malachy	Gold Dinky of Arcady	D. Rossitar	D. Rossitar	17.5.62
Golden Buttons of Yadnum	B	Emperor of Yadnum	Bonny Blue of Yadnum	Mrs E. Munday	Mrs E. Munday	7.5.61

Name of Champion	Sex	Sire	Dam	Breeder	Owner	Date of Birth
1965						
Anston Cindy Loo	B	Anston Blue Emperor	Alfeebas Joy	Mrs A.L. Buxton	Mrs Moore	29.2.60
My Precious Joss	D	Ch. Primbron of Johnstounburn	Bonney Jean	Mrs C. Flockhart	Mrs C. Flockhart	21.2.63
Ruswell Chorus Girl of Brendali	B	Ch. Glamour Boy of Glengonner	Mandy of Glengonner	Mr D.A. Peck	Mrs R. Marshall	20.8.62
Tempervale Niaissmo of Wiske	B	Tempervale Benissimo	Tempervale Lady Monia	Mrs H. Briggs	Mrs K.M. Renton	11.7.63
Viada Rosina	B	Wylhylad Tiny Tim	Sadie of Invincia	Mrs V.A. Monger	Mrs V.A. Monger	15.8.63
Wedgwood Starmist	D	Fair Victor of Clu-Mor	Wedgwood's Vickie	Mrs C.L. Morris	Mrs M. Logue	4.5.62
Whisperdales Phirno Carmen	B	Ch. Ravelin Gaiety Boy	Blue Biddy	Miss P.I. Noakes	Mr R. Wardell	26.2.63
1966						
Carlwyns Wee Teddy Toff	D	Ch. Stirkeans Astonoffs Horatio	Stirkeans Cherry Ripe	Mrs W.E. Nichols	Mrs W.E. Nichols	7.10.63
Phirno St George	D	Ravelin Little Jimmy	Phirno Dawn Delight	Miss P. Noakes	Miss P. Noakes	23.4.64
Skyrona Blue Girl	B	Ch. Skyrona Blue Prince	Woldsdene Blue Rose	Mrs G. Sykes	Mrs G. Sykes	22.6.64
Templevale Jessica of Wiske	B	Templevale Simonson	Templevale Giselle	Mrs L.H. Briggs	Mrs K.M. Renton	17.10.64
Beechrise Superb	D	Ch. Pagnell Peter Pan	Beechrise Pixie	Mrs H. Griffiths	Mrs H. Griffiths	5.8.63
Dorrits Leyham Scampi	D	Leyham Tuppence	Leyham Starbright	Mrs D. Mayall	Mrs D. Baynes	19.11.62
Progresso Pearl	B	Progresso Melody	Fairmead Jane	Mr Brown	Mrs C. Hutchin	2.7.64
Lillyhill Primbronette	B	Ch. Primbron of Johnstounburn	Fair Blossom	Mr W. Dores	Mrs W. Wilson	12.3.62
Stirkeans Reenie	B	Ch. Stirkeans Astonoffs Horatio	Stirkeans Romance	Mrs E. Stirk	Mrs E. Stirk	2.4.65
Progresso Prospect	D	Ch. Progresso Lover Boy	Topsy Jane	Mr Langley	Mrs C. Hutchin	4.1.64

Name of Champion	Sex	Sire	Dam	Breeder	Owner	Date of Birth
1967						
Burantheas Luscious Lady	B	Burantheas Ben Braggie	Burantheas Prime Mover	Mrs H.D. Burfield	Mrs H.D. Burfield	1.8.63
Blairsville Tinkerbell	B	Leodian Smart Boy	Blairsville Lady	Mr & Mrs Lister	Mr & Mrs Lister	7.9.65
Dorrits Susanne's Treasure	B	Ch. Burantheas Saint Malachy	Ch. My Sweet Susan	Mrs D. Baynes	Mrs D. Baynes	10.10.65
Heavenly Blue of Wiske	D	Ch. Pagnell Peter Pan	Ch. Doone of Wiske	Mrs K.M. Renton	Mr & Mrs Palframan	28.2.63
Skyrona Blue Bobby of Streamglen	D	Ch. Skyrona Blue Prince	Enchanted Lady of Rosehara	Mrs G. Sykes	Mrs M. Waldram	2.3.65
Macstroud's Sir Gay	D	Ch. Carlwyns Wee Teddy Toff	Macstroud's Little Nell	Mr D. Stroud	Mr D. Stroud	15.1.66
Blue Flash of Streamglen	D	Wee Tich of Streamglen	Fifi Petite	Mrs Marsden	Mrs M. Waldram	3.6.65
Pagnell Blue Peter	D	Ch. Pagnell Peter Pan	Issobel Lady	Mrs D. Smith	Mrs S.I. Groom	4.4.64
Anston Lucy Locket	B	Anston Scampy Gem	Anston Slaay	Mrs Moore	Mrs Moore	28.9.64
Stirkeans Gerrards Little Guy	D	Ch. Stirkeans Astonoffs Horatio	Blairsville Lady	Mr & Mrs B. Lister	Mr & Mrs B. Lister	13.7.66
1968						
Chantmarles Mycariad Wild Silk	B	Macstroud's Whitecross Dandini	Mycariad Astonoff Lady Virginia	Miss M.V. Childs	Mrs M. Hayes	16.8.66
Dandini Jim	D	Ch. Beechrise Superb	Little Enchantress	Mr B. Blamires	Mr B. Blamires	1.11.65
Deebees Doncella	B	Deebees Tommy Tucker	Deebees Sweet Celeste	Mr D. Beech	Mr D. Beech	14.6.66
Luna Star of Yadnum	D	Bright Star of Yadnum	Bonny Blue of Yadnum	Mrs E. Munday	Mrs E. Munday	7.8.65
Murose Storm	D	Ch. Beechrise Superb	Murose Sherrie	Mrs E. Burton	Mrs E. Burton	21.8.66
Tolcarne Brandy Soda	D	Lambsgrove Pinnochio	Tolcarne Grenbar Kanzette	Mrs O. Wood	Mrs O. Wood	28.6.65
Whisperdales Temujin	D	Ravelin Little Jimmy	Ch. Whisperdales Phirno Carmen	Mrs R. Wardell	Mr R. Wardell	8.11.66

Name of Champion	Sex	Sire	Dam	Breeder	Owner	Date of Birth
1969						
Blairsville Boy Wonder	D	Leodian Smart Boy	Blairsville Lady	Mr & Mrs B. Lister	Mr & Mrs B. Lister	13.7.66
Bobby of Beachdale	D	Little Gay Boy of Beechrise	Janette of Beachdale	Mrs A.M. Beach	Mrs A.M. Beach	9.9.67
Chantmarles Snuff Box	B	Macstrouds Whitecross Dandini	Mycariad Stargazer	Mrs M.C. Hayes	Mrs M.C. Hayes	31.10.68
Deanchel's Beau Caprice	D	Ozmilion Nobel Boy	Deanchel's Sukis Blue Caprice	Mrs E. Taylor	Mrs E. Taylor	10.2.68
Deebees Gold Penny	B	Deebees Gold Plum	Ch. Deebees Little Dodo	Mrs D. Beech	Mrs D. Beech	13.2.67
Elspeth Serenade	B	Elspeth Wonder Boy	Kelsbro Moonbean	Miss E. Lomas & Miss E. Pass	Miss E. Lomas & Miss E. Pass	8.3.66
Macstroud's High Society	B	Int. Ch. Macstroud's Sir Gay	Macstroud's Jacks Memory	Mr D. Stroud	Mr D. Stroud	3.1.68
Nelmila Berryfield Beauty	D	Chunky of Archombeaux	Whitecross Mitzi	Mrs I.M. Millard	Mrs I.M. Millard	10.9.64
Newholme Marco Polo	D	Wee Boy Blue	Beechrise Pixie	W.K. Cherryholme	W.K. Cherryholme	12.2.65
Pretty Debbie of Yadnum	B	Bright Star of Yadnum	Fair Phillipa	Mrs G. Bulgin	Miss V. Munday	10.12.66
Star of Keith	D	Sketrick Shi-Shi-Bu	Sketrick Sharon Rose	Mr Gardner	Mrs I. Copley	18.9.68
Tayfirs Firegift	D	Mr Teddy of Phylreyne	Rose of Reenad	Mrs Fairbrother	Mrs J. Fairbrother	18.8.65
1970						
Blairsville Aristocrat	D	Ch. Beechrise Superb	Ch. Blairsville Tinkerbell	Mr & Mrs B. Lister	Mr & Mrs B. Lister	11.9.68
Blairsville Shirene	B	Ch. Blairsville Boy Wonder	Blairsville Belinda	Mr & Mrs B. Lister	Mr & Mrs B. Lister	29.9.67
Elspeth Nina of Ravaldene	B	Kelsbro Top Choice of Sweetloves	Elspeth Snee Susy	Miss E. Lomas & Miss P. Pass	Mr V. Ravald	1.6.67
Lyndoney Timothy Tuppence	D	Little Master of Hilfore	Lyndoney Tina Marie	Mrs E.C. Johnson	Mrs E.C. Johnson	27.6.67

Name of Champion	Sex	Sire	Dam	Breeder	Owner	Date of Birth
Macstroud's Noble Lad	D	Int. Ch. Macstroud's Sir Gay	Plantation Hall Susan of Wiske	Mr D. Stroud	Mr D. Stroud	1.2.69
Murose Wee Pippa	D	Ch. Murose Storm	Murose Blue Dawn	Mrs E. Burton	Mrs E. Burton	13.6.68
Skyrona Blue Victoria	B	Ch. Beechrise Superb	Ch. Skyrona Blue Girl	Mrs Sykes	Mr Sykes	15.11.68
Super Fine of Yadnum	D	Star of Yadnum	Gay Rosalinda of Yadnum	Miss V. Munday	Miss V. Munday	10.7.68
Wydebank Super Solitaire	B	Pagnell Pandarus	Wydebank Debutante	Mr B. Blamire	Mr B. Blamire	10.5.68
1971						
Dorrit's Macstroud's Hot Toddy	D	Macstroud's Whitecross Dandini	Macstroud's Mitzi	Mr D. Stroud	Mrs D. Baynes	9.1.67
Wydebank Amethyst	B	Ch. Murose Storm	Wydebank Emma Peel	Mr A. Blamires	Mr A. Blamires	28.3.69
Gaykeys Gold	D	Gaykeys Firecracker	Gaykeys Sorreldene Lucy Locket	J. & M. Hesketh	J. & M. Hesketh	19.7.68
Ravaldene Graybet Rhapsody in Blue	B	Graybet Master Mike	Graybet Blue Rose	Mr & Mrs Mitchell	Mr V. Ravald	8.9.69
Brave Warrior of Naylenor	D	Ch. Heavenly Blue of Wiske	Sombrero Daisy May	Mr P. Naylor	Mr P. Naylor	18.5.69
Chantmarles Boniface	B	Macstroud's Whitecross Dandini	Mycariad Stargazer	Mrs M. Hayes	Mrs M. Hayes	17.2.68
Tolcarne Drambuie	D	Ch. Brandy Soda	Tolcarne Blue Rain	Mrs O. Wood	Mrs O. Wood	2.12.68
Blairsville Samantha	B	Ch. Blairsville Boy Wonder	Blairsville Belinda	Mr & Mrs B. Lister	Mr & Mrs B. Lister	5.6.70
Deebees Beebee	B	Deebees Bumble Boy	Wee Polly Fisher of Shipton	Mrs Picher	Mrs D. Beech	7.7.69
1972						
Mycariad Ragged Robin of Yadnum	D	Mycariad Tam O'Shanter	Mycariad Merry Go Round	Miss V. Childs	Miss V. Munday	20.1.70
Beechrise Surprise	D	Ch. Beechrise Superb	Jane Cutler	Mrs E. Dean	Mrs H. Griffiths	2.8.70

Name of Champion	Sex	Sire	Dam	Breeder	Owner	Date of Birth
Deanchel's Prince Pericles	D	Ch. Whisperdales Tamujin	Deanchels Sukis Blue Caprice	Mrs E. Taylor	Mrs E. Taylor	25.4.70
Ozmilion My Imagination	D	Ch. Blairsville Aristocrat	Ozmilion Tender Moment	Mr O. Sameja	Mr O. Sameja	14.7.70
Foxclose Little John	D	American Ch. Fuss Pot	Foxclose Blue Jean	Mr D.M. Jackson	Mrs D.M. Jackson	22.6.70
Kellaylys Miss Sophie	B	Chunky of Archambaud	Kellaylys Ramleaze Mighty Atom	Mrs Kellar	Mr J. Thrupp	18.4.70
Murose Exquisite	B	Ch. Murose Wee Pippa	Murose Delight	Mrs E. Burton	Mrs E. Burton	9.9.70
Whisperdales Deebees Halfpenny	B	Ch. Whisperdales Tamujin	Ch. Deebees Gold Penny	Mrs D. Beech	Mr W. Wardell	12.5.70
1973						
Lloyslee Lass	B	Simon Stroller	Oxcarr Dinkie	Mr E. Lloyd	Mr E. Lloyd	20.4.71
Phirno Lord Gay	D	Deebees Sunbeam	Phirno Rosie	Miss P. Noakes	Miss P. Noakes	11.4.71
Ozmilion Jubilation	D	Ch. Ozmilion My Imagination	Ozmilion Justine	Mr O. Sameja	Mr O. Sameja	4.10.71
Finstal Sugar Baby	B	Skyrona Blue Boy	Streamglen Beatrice	Mrs Pritchard	Mrs Pritchard	24.2.72
Wykebank Impeccable	B	Beechrise Splendid	Wykebank Debutante	Mr A. Blamires	Mr A. Blamires	14.7.71
Macstroud's Noble Boy	D	Ch. Macstroud's Sir Gay	Chantmarles Miss Silk	Mr D. Stroud	Mr D. Stroud	4.10.71
Blairsville Most Royal	B	Ch. Whisperdales Tamujin	Ch. Blairsville Shirene	Mr & Mrs B. Lister	Mr & Mrs B. Lister	12.5.71
Candytops Blue Peter	D	Candytops Deebees Peter Piper	Candytops Pandora	Mr & Mrs Oakley	Mr & Mrs Oakley	3.6.71
Brascaysh Bezzer of Murose	D	Ch. Murose Wee Pippa	Macstroud's Sunshine	Mrs M. Pritchard	Mrs E. Burton	23.6.71
Chantmarles Saucebox	D	Ch. Macstroud's Sir Gay	Ch. Chantmarles Snuffbox	Mrs M.C. Hayes	Mrs M.C. Hayes	3.5.71
1974						
Myork Muffin	D	Carlwyns Wee John	Modern Morita	Mrs K. Kemp	Mrs K. Kemp	22.10.71
Jackread Whisky A Go Go Stewell	D	Ravelin Little Jimmy	Jackread Cara Tina	Mrs J. Reader	Mr & Mrs Bardwell	19.8.71

Name of Champion	Sex	Sire	Dam	Breeder	Owner	Date of Birth
Ozmilion Modesty	B	Int. Ch. Ozmilion Jubilation	Ozmilion Blairsville Bidene	Mr O. Sameja	Mr O. Sameja	14.4.73
Foxclose Mr Smartie	D	Ch. Foxclose Little John	Foxclose Peggy O'Neill	Mrs M. Jackson	Mrs M. Jackson	26.1.72
Deebees Cornish Echo	D	Deebees Cock Robin	Deebees Caromies Carrisima	Mrs D. Beech	Mrs D. Beech	2.10.72
Chantmarles Sashbox	B	Ch. Chantmarles Saucebox	Ch. Chantmarles Miss Boniface	Mrs M. Hayes	Mrs M. Hayes	16.6.72
Robina Gay of Yadnum	B	Ch. Mycariad Ragged Robin of Yadnum	Gay Roslina of Yadnum	Miss V. Munday	Miss V. Munday	14.4.71
Pegles Salamander	B	Ch. Beechrise Surprise	Pegles Mon Cherie	Mrs P. Foster	Mrs P. Foster	12.9.72
Kelaylys Master Tino	D	Chunky of Archombeaux	Kellaylys Ramleaze Mighty Atom	Mrs G. Kellar	Mrs G. Kellar	4.7.72
1975						
Gerjoy Royal Flea	D	Ch. Beechrise Superb	Lambsgrove Messalina	Mr G.A. Wattam	Mr G.A. Wattam	9.4.72
Clarebecks Moonraker	D	Ch. Chantmarles Saucebox	Clarebecks Candy Mint	Mrs J. Hughes	Mrs J. Hughes	9.11.72
Harleta Uno Go Go	D	Ch. Whisperdales Tamujin	Harleta Precious Jocelyne	Mrs L. Hilton	Mrs L. Hilton	9.5.73
Carmardy Little Henry	D	Carmardy Captain Kydd	Lady Lisa of Abbeydale Carmardy	Mr & Mrs H.P. Parkin	Mr & Mrs H.P. Parkin	18.4.73
Deebees Penny Rose	D	Ch. Deebees Cornish Echo	Ch. Deebees Gold Penny	Mrs D. Beech	Mrs D. Beech	1.7.73
Garsims Moonshine	B	Candytops Cornelius	Babette of Index	Mrs P. Rose	Mrs P. Rose	14.5.73
Naylenor Blue Monarch	D	Ch. Brave Warrior Naylenor	Wydebank Gaiety Girl	Mr P. Naylor	Mr P. Naylor	30.4.72
Lyndoney Krishna	D	Ch. Dorrit's Macstroud's Hot Toddy	Lyndoney Suzetta	Mrs D. Johnson	Mrs D. Johnson	11.11.72

Name of Champion	Sex	Sire	Dam	Breeder	Owner	Date of Birth
Ebracum Paladin	D	Ebracum Priam	Ebracum Gem	Mr J.R. Haynes	Mr J.R. Haynes	15.4.73
Swank of Beechrise	D	Beechrise Splendour	Thatchcroft Superb Kate	Mrs Marshall	Mrs H. Griffiths	14.1.73
Blairsville Royal Seal	D	Ch. Beechrise Surprise	Ch. Blairsville Most Royale	Mr & Mrs B. Lister	Mr & Mrs B. Lister	2.5.74
Macstroud's Soldier Blue	D	Int. Ch. Macstroud's Noble Lad	Macstroud's Society Girl	Mr D. Stroud	Mr D. Stroud	26.7.73
1976						
Kattefare of Candytops	B	Candytops Cornelius	Lansfield Lass	Mr F. Morris	Mr & Mrs Oakley	9.2.74
Ozmilion Justimagine	B	Ch. Ozmilion My Imagination	Ozmilion Blairsville Bidene	Mr O. Sameja	Mr O. Sameja	3.3.75
Empress of Murose	B	Ch. Murose Wee Pippa	Thornhaw Lady Gipsy	Mrs M. Holmes	Mrs E. Burton	2.9.74
Toy Top Tango	B	Ch. Beechrise Superb	Toy Top Topsy	Mrs D. Kitchen	Mrs D. Kitchen	8.3.73
Candytops Chantilly Lace	B	Ch. Candytops Blue Peter	Candytops Clarissa	Mr & Mrs Oakley	Mr & Mrs Oakley	30.11.73
Ozmilion Destiny	B	Int. Ch. Ozmilion Jubilation	Ozmilion Winter Goddess	Mr O. Sameja	Mrs Montgomery	26.7.74
1977						
Paglea Con Tutto	D	Ch. Chantmarles Sauce Box	Paglea Mon Cherie	Mrs P. Foster	Mrs P. Foster	14.11.73
Ozmilion Distinction	D	Int. Ch. Ozmilion Jubilation	Ozmilion Summer Illusion	Mr O. Sameja	Mr O. Sameja	5.5.75
Ozmilion Dream Maker	B	Int. Ch. Ozmilion Jubilation	Ozmilion Tickle	Mr O. Sameja	Mrs V. Sameja-Williams	15.11.74
Leadmore Lady Angela	B	Leadmore Tiny Sparkle	Leadmore Blue Sapphire	Mr W. Cusack	Mr W. Cusack	12.8.75
Chantmarles Elegance	B	Ch. Chantmarles Sauce Box	Chantmarles Nelmila Briar Rose	Mrs M.C. Hayes	Mrs M.C. Hayes	3.2.75
Ozmilion Premonition	D	Ch. Ozmilion Distinction	Ch. Ozmilion Justimagine	Mr O. Sameja	Mr O. Sameja	1.8.76

Name of Champion	Sex	Sire	Dam	Breeder	Owner	Date of Birth
Wykebank Startime	B	Ch. Blairsville Royal Startime	Wykebank Twinkle Star	Mr A. Blamire	Mr A. Blamire	12.2.76
Deebees Speculation	D	Deebees Dancing Dan	Deebees Pennys Sunshine	Mrs S.D. Beech	Mrs S.D. Beech	21.8.75
Craigsbank Blue Cinders	B	Southwardedge Blue Spark	Craigsbank Sweet Kandy	Mrs J. Mann	Mrs J. Mann	30.1.76
Julliette Bradstara	B	Ch. Foxclose Mr Smartie	Mistywinkle Bell	Mrs Kitching	Mr & Mrs Bradshaw	26.3.75
Chevawn Sweet Shona	B	Mogid Whata Charmer from Chevawn	Astolats Jasmine	Mrs J. Campion	Mrs E. Layton & Mrs S. Chiswell	28.3.76
Candytops Strawberry Fayre	B	Ch. Candytops Blue Peter	Sophie of Candytops	Mr & Mrs H. Oakley	Mr & Mrs H. Oakley	29.6.75
1978						
Shaun of Beechrise	D	Speculation of Beechrise	Two Pennorth of Copper	Mrs P. Gray	Mrs H. Griffiths	29.6.75
Typros Evening Star	B	Cheeky Boy Typros	Macstroud's Evening Star	Mrs Da Silva	Mrs Da Silva	17.1.74
Verolian Justajule with Ozmilion	D	Int. Ch. Jubilation	Ozmilion Wild Temptress	Mrs V. Sameja-Hilliard	Mrs V. Sameja-Hilliard	28.2.76
Ozmilion Exageration	B	Ch. Ozmilion My Imagination	Int. Ch. Ozmilion Modesty	Mr O. Sameja	Mr O. Sameja	13.9.76
Jackread Apple Blossom	D	Jackread Jiminy Cricket	Misstress Emma of Jackread	Mrs J. Reader	Mrs J. Reader	25.3.76
Wellshim Madam of Deebees	D	Deebees Oberon	Dainty Dinah of Wellshim	Mrs A. Shinwell	Mrs Beech & Mrs A. Shinwell	25.12.75
Typros The Devil of Spice Box	D	Chantmarles Spice Box	Snowdrop of Typros	Mrs G. Da Silva	Mrs G. Da Silva	14.7.75
Naylenor Magic Moment	B	Naylenor Battle Cry	Naylenor Honey Bunny	Mr & Mrs P. Naylor	Mr & Mrs P. Naylor	3.12.76
Candytops Raffles	D	Ch. Candytops Blue Peter	Melody Fair of Candytops	Mr & Mrs H. Oakley	Mr & Mrs H. Oakley	12.11.76

Name of Champion	Sex	Sire	Dam	Breeder	Owner	Date of Birth
1979						
Fascination of Daisydell	D	Daisydell Midsummer Lad	Miss Tina of Heymor	Mr G. Taylor & Miss S. Morelli	Mr & Mrs M. Turner	23.3.77
Chantmarles Debutante	B	Chantmarles Tartar Sauce	Chantmarles Briar Rose	Mrs M. Hayes	Mr P. Booth	8.8.76
Ozmilion Tradition	D	Ch. Ozmilion Premonition	Ch. Ozmilion Exageration	Mr O. Sameja	Mr O. Sameja	1.1.78
Wykebank Wild Rose	B	Ch. Blairsville Royal Seal	Wykebank Twinkle Star	Mr A. Blamires	Mrs K. Henderson	12.2.76
Carmardy Marcus	D	Captain Kydd of Carmardy	Carmardy Little Lille	Mr & Mrs H. Parkin	Mr & Mrs H. Parkin	1.3.77
Chantmarles Dolly Dimple	B	Ch. Chantmarles Stowaway	Chantmarles Maggiemay	Mrs M. Hayes	Mrs M. Hayes	3.6.77
Deebees My Fascination	D	Deebees Dancing Dan	Ch. Wellshim Madam of Deebees	Mrs D. Beech	Mrs D. Beech & Mrs A. Shinwell	12.3.76
Harleta Ferdinando	D	Evenwood Ambassador	Chantmarles Rose Bud	Mr & Mrs L. Hilton	Mr & Mrs L. Hilton	12.3.76
Beechrise Sweet Solitaire	B	Ch. Swank of Beechrise	Sundae of Beechrise	Mrs H. Griffiths	Mr & Mrs D. Sargenson	13.10.76
Chantmarles Stowaway	D	Chantmarles Tartar Sauce	Chantmarles Cress	Mrs M. Hayes	Mrs M. Hayes	18.4.76
Ozmilion Hearts Desire	B	Ch. Ozmilion Premonition	Swed. Ch. Justaromance	Mr O. Sameja	Mr O. Sameja	3.1.78
1980						
Daisydell Tinker	D	Daisydell Midsummer Lad	Daisydell Spring Juill	Mr & Mrs W. Kneen	Mr & Mrs W. Kneen	24.8.77
Mogid Millionairess	B	Ch. Ozmilion Premonition	Mogid Just Dolly	Mrs M. Gidding	Mrs M. Gidding	1.9.77
Craigsbank Miss Dior	B	Southwardedge Blue Spark of Craigsbank	Craigsbank Sweet Nanette	Mrs J.W. Mann	Mrs J.W. Mann	10.9.77
Souvenir of Beechrise	D	Ch. Shaun of Beechrise	Coletts Cheeky Debbie	Mrs M. Cole	Mrs H. Griffiths	16.10.77

Name of Champion	Sex	Sire	Dam	Breeder	Owner	Date of Birth
Ozmilion Devotion	D	Ch. Ozmilion Premonition	Ch. Ozmilion Justimagine	Mr O. Sameja	Mr O. Sameja	5.6.78
Wykebank Tinkerbell	B	Blairsville Royal Monarch	Wykebank Vanity Fair	Mr A. Blamire	Mr A. Blamire	24.2.78
Chantmarles Proper Madam	B	Ch. Chantmarles Stowaway	Chantmarles Inis Cara	Mrs M. Hayes	Mrs M. Hayes	7.5.78
Deebees Golden Delight	B	Deebees Othello	Barlizsue Ee Emma	Mrs D. Beech & Mrs Shinwell	Mrs D. Beech & Mrs Shinwell	27.7.78
Blairsville Gaiety Boy	D	Blairsville Royal Monarch	Blairsville Dream Girl	Mr & Mrs B. Lister	Mr & Mrs B. Lister	5.10.78
Murose Illustrious	D	Ebracum Pimento of Murose	Murose Merry Go Round	Mrs E. Burton	Mrs E. Burton	15.11.76
Candytops Candy Man	D	Ch. Candytops Blue Peter	Candytops Florence	Mr & Mrs Oakley	Mr & Mrs Oakley	3.12.77
Ozmilion Ovation	D	Ch. Ozmilion Tradition	Ch. Ozmilion Hearts Desire	Mr O. Sameja	Mr O. Sameja	11.1.79
1981						
Ozmilion Story of Romance	B	Ch. Ozmilion Devotion	Ch. Ozmilion Exageration	Mr O. Sameja	Mr O. Sameja	25.6.79
Johnalena Silken Charm	D	Ch. Ozmilion Distinction	Nelmila Berryfield Justine	Mrs K. John	Mrs K. John	30.10.78
Finstal Johnathan	D	Garsims Captain Moonshine	Finstal Evita	Mrs S. Pritchard	Mrs S. Pritchard	9.3.79
Marshonia Blue Secret	D	Marshonia Inspiration	Marshonia Love Story	Mrs P. Robson	Mrs P. Robson	5.3.79
Candytops Fair Delight	B	Ch. Candytops Cavalcadia	Ch. Katie Fare of Candytops	Mr & Mrs Oakley	Mr & Mrs Oakley	10.5.79
Murose Masterpiece	D	Murose Illustrious	Madam Murose	Mrs E. Burton	Mrs E. Burton	29.9.79
Candytops Cavalcadia	D	Ch. Blairsville Royal Seal	Ch. Candytops Chantilly Lace	Mr & Mrs Oakley	Mr & Mrs Oakley	3.12.77
Chandas Shonas Girl	B	Ch. Ozmilion Distinction	Ch. Chevawn Sweet Shona	Mrs E. Leyton & Mrs S. Chiswell	Mrs E. Leyton & Mrs S. Chiswell	19.11.78

Name of Champion	Sex	Sire	Dam	Breeder	Owner	Date of Birth
Franbrin Royal Sapphire of Woodcross	B	Franbrin Royal Admiral	Chiquita of Vandepere	Mrs F. Thorley	Mrs J. Mills	14.3.78
Chantmarles Rose Bowl	B	Ch. Chantmarles Saucebox	Chantmarles Isadora	Mrs M. Hayes	Mrs D. Lorenz	22.6.75
Chantmarles Celebrity	D	Int. Ch. Ozmilion Jubilation	Chantmarles Maggiemay	Mrs M. Hayes	Mrs M. Hayes	2.1.80
Summer Sensation of Sedae	B	Ch. Ozmilion Distinction	Miti Pito of Kumar	Miss E. Silva	Mrs M. Eades	10.5.79

1982

Name of Champion	Sex	Sire	Dam	Breeder	Owner	Date of Birth
Stewell Moonstorm	D	Ch. Jackread Whisky-A-Go-Go Stewell	Alvin Cindy Mac of Stewell	Mrs E. Bardwell	Mrs E. Bardwell	24.6.79
Wykebank Star Choice	B	Wykebank Wonder Boy	Wykebank Starshine	Mr A. Blamire	Mr A. Blamire	27.9.79
Shipps Shanty Mann	D	Drummer Boy of Shipps	Shipps Truly Fair	Mrs M. Hamill	Mrs M. Hamill	7.9.79
Moseville Misty Lady of Hankeyville	B	Star of Beechrise	Golden Madonna	Mrs M. Tracy	Mrs Hanforth	12.7.80
Chantmarles Best Intentions	D	Int. Ch. Ozmilion Jubilation	Ch. Chantmarles Dolly Dimple	Mrs M. Hayes	Mrs M. Hayes	7.11.80
Ozmilion Flames of Desire	B	Int. Ch. Ozmilion Jubilation	Ch. Ozmilion Exageration	Mr O. Sameja	Mr O. Sameja	12.1.81
Relation of Primemeadows	D	Primemeadows Sophist	Bransholme Peppe	Mrs Wright	Mrs Robinson	2.7.80
Craigsbank Stormy Affair	B	Craigsbank Sirius	Craigsbank Stephanie	Mrs J.W. Mann	Mrs J. Leslie	20.2.80
Jamesons Royal Stewart	D	Ch. Blairsville Royal Seal	Jamesons Blue Fascination	Mr & Mrs Henderson	Mr & Mrs Henderson	18.4.80
Ozmilion Expectation	D	Ch. Ozmilion Ovation	Ch. Ozmilion Story of Romance	Mrs O. Sameja	Mrs O. Sameja	14.7.80
Deebees Dominic	D	Deebees Oberon	Quiberon Dominique	Mrs Beech & Mrs Shinwell	Mrs Beech & Mrs Shinwell	9.10.80

Name of Champion	Sex	Sire	Dam	Breeder	Owner	Date of Birth
Sharwins Easter Dream	B	Ch. Ozmilion Distinction	Bo Peep of Sharwin	Mr D. Baldwin	Mr D. Baldwin	15.4.79
Chantmarles Wild Rose	B	Ch. Foxclose Mr Smartie	Chantmarles Isadora	Mrs M. Hayes	Mrs D. Lorenz	28.10.78
Ozmilion Flames of Passion	B	Ch. Ozmilion Devotion	Ch. Ozmilion Destiny	Mr O. Sameja	Mr O. Sameja	5.11.80
Verolian Temptress with Ozmilion	B	Int. Ch. Ozmilion Jubilation	Ozmilion Love Story	Mrs V. Sameja-Hilliard	Mrs V. Sameja-Hilliard	18.9.80
Wenwytes Whisper Boy	D	Ch. Candytops Cavalcadia	Wenwytes Winter Whisper	Mrs W. White	Mrs W. White	24.4.80

1983

Name of Champion	Sex	Sire	Dam	Breeder	Owner	Date of Birth
Kindonia Justin	D	Int. Ch. Ozmilion Jubilation	Kindonia Premier Girl	Mr & Mrs G. Briddon	Mr & Mrs G. Briddon	25.2.81
Ozmilion Love Romance	B	Ch. Ozmilion Tradition	Ch. Ozmilion Hearts Desire	Mr O. Sameja	Mr O. Sameja	3.4.81
Arlestry Regal Challenge	D	Ch. Blairsville Royal Seal	Arlestry Memorie Cherie	Mrs E. Howarth	Mrs E. Howarth	23.9.79
Ozmilion Invitation	D	Ch. Ozmilion Expectation	Ch. Ozmilion Exageration	Mr O. Sameja	Mr O. Sameja	20.2.82
Bee Bee Mi Blaze	B	Ch. Blairsville Royal Seal	Heidi of Peppinoville of Bee Bee Mi	Mrs J. Mitchell	Mr J.A. Magri	11.5.79
Candytops Royal Cascade	D	Ch. Candytops Cavalcadia	Candytops Ribbons Delight	Mr & Mrs H. Oakley	Mr & Mrs H. Oakley	13.2.81
Ozmilion Dance of Romance	B	Int. Ch. Ozmilion Jubilation	Ch. Ozmilion Story of Romance	Mr O. Sameja	Mr O. Sameja	29.7.81
Mondamin My Minstrele	B	Ch. Ozmilion Tradition	Mondamin Endeavour	Mrs I. Dawson	Mrs I. Dawson	25.4.80
Azurene Moss Rose of Yadnum	B	Yadnum Star Touch	Yadnum Love Joy of Azurene	Mrs G. Bulgin	Mrs G. Bulgin	26.5.80
Typros Royal Splendour	D	Ch. Swank of Beechrise	Typros Rewards	Mrs G. Da Silva	Mrs G. Da Silva	29.10.81

Name of Champion	Sex	Sire	Dam	Breeder	Owner	Date of Birth
Emotions of Ozmilion at Rozamie	D	Ch. Swank of Beechrise	Minetown Bluebell	Mrs Hanforth	Mr J. Magri	9.11.81
Naejekin Blue Reflection	D	Naejekin Blue Flint	Naejekin Anita	Mr M. Bebbington	Mrs E. Carr	20.11.81
Evening Blue	D	Naejekin Blue Flint	Blairsville Sue Ellen	Mr & Mrs Gillespie	Mr & Mrs Gillespie	5.6.82
Coletts Charmaine	B	Ch. Ozmilion Ovation	Coletts Princess	Mrs M. Cole	Mrs M. Cole	1.1.82
Stewells Soul Singer	B	Stewell Sensation	Stewell Tinkerbell	Mr S. & Mrs E. Bardwell	Mr S. & Mrs E. Bardwell	21.2.82
Blairsville Royal Pardon	B	Blairsville Royal Monarch	Blairsville Royal Destiny	Mr & Mrs B. Lister	Mr & Mrs Gillespie	22.9.81
Chantmarles Candy	B	Ch. Chantmarles Stowaway	Chantmarles Bella Paula	Mrs M. Hayes	Mr & Mrs R. Haythornthwaite	2.10.79
1985						
Ozmilion Hopelessly In Love	B	Ch. Ozmilion Distinction	Ch. Ozmilion Flames of Desire	Mr O. Sameja	Mr O. Sameja	6.4.83
Taurusdale Pilinan Hati	D	Kelleyly's Master Tristram	Taurusdale Tender Touch	Mr D. Kee	Mr D. Kee	1.7.82
Naylenor Crown Jewel	D	Ch. Candytops Cavalcadia	Naylenor Regal Rose	Mr & Mrs P. Naylor	Mr & Mrs P. Naylor	18.8.82
Craigsbank Sheezalady	B	Craigsbank King of Hearts	Craigsbank Romance	Mrs J.W. Mann	Mrs J. Leslie	1.6.82
Marshonia Secret Serenade	B	Marshonia Startrek	Marshonia Love Affair	Mrs P. Robinson	Mrs P. Robinson	3.6.83
Azurene Corduroy of Yadnum	D	Yadnum Star Touch	Yadnum Love Joy of Azurene	Mrs G. Bulgin	Miss V. Munday	23.7.81
Maritoys Midnight Rose	B	Lyndoney Little Cracker of Maritoys	Jerina's Briar Rose of Maritoys	Mrs M. Watton	Mrs J. Blamire	17.3.83
Marshonia Top Secret	D	Ch. Marshonia Blue Secret	Marshonia My Precious Claire	Mr P. Robinson	Mr & Mrs Parker	29.11.80
Verolian Appreciation at Ozmilion	D	Ch. Ozmilion Distinction	Verolian Theme on a Dream at Ozmilion	Mrs V. Sameja-Hilliard	Mrs V. Sameja-Hilliard	12.9.82
Carmardy Cassius	D	Ch. Ozmilion Expectation	Carmardy Angelena	Mrs J. Parkin	Mrs J. Parkin	20.11.83

Name of Champion	Sex	Sire	Dam	Breeder	Owner	Date of Birth
1986						
Ozmilion Admiration	D	Ch. Ozmilion Invitation	Ch. Ozmilion Love Romance	Mr O. Sameja	Mr O. Sameja	24.8.83
Polliam Sweet Delight	B	Int. Ch. Ozmilion Jubilation	Polliam Sweet Destiny	Mrs P. Osborne	Mrs P. Osborne	5.7.82
Shianda Royal Fanfare	D	Deebees Orthello	Shianda Cara Cree	Mrs S. Davies	Mrs S. Davies	18.1.83
Ozmilion Kisses of Fire	B	Ch. Ozmilion Expectation	Ch. Ozmilion Hearts Desire	Mr O. Sameja	Mr O. Sameja	1.8.84
Christmas Fable	B	Ch. Ozmilion Distinction	Fatal Charm	Mr & Mrs Gillespie	Mr & Mrs Gillespie	16.12.83
Keriwell Flirtation	B	Int. Ch. Ozmilion Jubilation	Karina Mine	Mr J. Wells	Mr J. Wells	10.9.83
Lovejoys Debonaire Dandy	D	Arlestry Haydons Majestic	Bevmells Lavender Blue	Mrs S. Schaeffer	Mrs S. Schaeffer	30.4.82
Ozmilion Dedication	D	Ch. Ozmilion Admiration	Ch. Ozmilion Hearts Desire	Mr O. Sameja	Mr O. Sameja	20.4.85
Verolian The Adventuress at Ozmilion	B	Ch. Verolian Justajule with Ozmilion	Verolian the Seductress at Ozmilion	Mrs V. Sameja-Hilliard	Mrs V. Sameja-Hilliard	21.1.85
Lena Alanah Snowdrop of Cyndahl	B	Chozebar Solara	Anna Bella Sunshine	Mrs M.K. Seara	Mrs E. Morris	10.2.82
Meadpark Silken Velvet	B	Meadpark Personality Plus	Meadpark Blue Blaize	Mr & Mrs Mulligan	Mr & Mrs Mulligan	18.8.84
Chandas Inspiration	D	Ch. Ozmilion Invitation	Ch. Chevawn Sweet Shona	Mrs E. Leyton & Mrs S. Chiswell	Mrs E. Leyton & Mrs S. Chiswell	3.1.84
1987						
Clantalon Contention	D	Meadpark Personality Plus	Nelmila Berryfield Opal	Mr & Mrs McKay	Mr & Mrs McKay	20.4.84

Name of Champion	Sex	Sire	Dam	Breeder	Owner	Date of Birth
Crosspins Royal Sovereign	B	Ch. Ozmilion Distinction	Finstal Mary Rose	Mr & Mrs Rigby	Mr & Mrs Rigby	23.4.84
Amnlion Love Letter	B	Ch. Ozmilion Distinction	Ozmilion Modern Romance	Mrs A. Swaine-Wise	Mrs J. Leslie	5.5.85
Slademark Sweet Allure	B	Int. Ch. Ozmilion Jubilation	Slademark Schisandra	Mrs J. Dunning	Mr & Mrs Burnsoll	7.1.84
Royalties Reflex	D	Ch. Ozmilion Distinction	Fatal Charm	Mr & Mrs Gillespie	Mrs Y. Windsor	8.1.85
Keriwell Reflection	D	Ch. Ozmilion Invitation	Keriwell Contessa	Mr & Mrs Wells	Mr & Mrs Wells	24.8.84
Deanhal Selina	B	Clantalon Adulation	Deanhal Scorcha	Mrs J. Halliday	Mrs J. Halliday	4.8.83
Chantmarles President of Yat	D	Chantmarles Billy Buttons	Chantmarles Lily Langtry	Mrs M. Hayes	Mr Enz & Mr Downey	12.1.84
Carmardy Annie	B	Ch. Carmardy Cassius	Carmardy Rose Mary	Mrs J. Parkin	Mrs J. Parkin	28.9.85
Chantmarles Curiosity	D	Am. Ch. Chantmarles Welsh Pageant	Chantmarles Chique	Mrs M. Hayes	Mrs M. Hayes	20.6.64
Tamiche of Tayfirs	B	Tayfirs Regal Steel	Juekei's Sian	Mrs J. Dalton	Mrs Fairbrother	9.6.84
Candytops Amelia Fair	B	Ch. Candytops Royal Cascade	Sophies Candytops	Mr & Mrs Oakley	Mr & Mrs Oakley	1.8.84
Candytops Royal Sovereign	D	Ch. Candytops Royal Cascade	Candytops Lady Levant	Mr & Mrs H. Oakley	Mr & Mrs H. Oakley	20.8.83
1988						
Ozmilion Sensation	D	Ch. Ozmilion Dedication	Ch. Ozmilion Love Romance	Mr O. Sameja	Mr O. Sameja	18.8.86
Kanandee Magic Moments	B	Ch. Candytops Royal Sovereign	Garsims May Be	Mrs D. Hurcombe	Mrs D. Hurcombe	28.1.86
Keriwell True Love	B	Ch. Ozmilion Invitation	Cindyette Lady Mine	Mr J. Wells	Mr & Mrs J. Clelland	24.12.84
Royal Silk	B	Jon Awyns Markie	Suki of Curzenhouse	Mr & Mrs G. Forster	Mr & Mrs P. Whittaker	16.10.85
Pittens Whisky Twinkle	D	Copperfines Whisky Mac	Gerardene Twinkle Star	Mrs H. Ridgwell	Mrs H. Ridgwell	14.9.85
Stradmore Samba	B	Stradmore Classie	Stradmore Bobbys Gire	Mrs G. Rowland	Mrs G. Rowland	21.2.82

Name of Champion	Sex	Sire	Dam	Breeder	Owner	Date of Birth
Typros Lady of Elegance	B	Typros Presentation	Massendeans Love In A Mist	Mrs Da Silva	Mrs Da Silva	1.1.87
Deebees Golden Fancy	B	Ch. Yadnum Regal Fare	Deebees Just a Fancy	Mrs D. Beech	Mrs D. Beech & Mrs A.C. Shinwell	18.5.86
Rozamie Endless Love	B	Ch. Ozmilion Dedication	Rozamie Careless Whisper	Mr J. Magri	Mr G. Downey & Mr R. Enz	1.6.86
1989						
Crosspins Royal Brigadier	D	Crosspins Gaye Chance	Crosspins Midnight Rose	Mr & Mrs J. Rigby	Mr & Mrs J. Rigby	11.9.85
Stewell Storm Queen	B	Ch. Stewell Moonstorm	Stewell Sweet Delight	S.E. & M. Bardwell	S.E. & M. Bardwell	24.1.87
Brybett Finesse	D	Brybett Dedication	Brybett Brambles	Mrs B. Whitbread	Mrs B. Whitbread	25.11.86
Bananas Du Domaine De Monderlay at Gaysteps	B	Sp. Ch. Royal Flash De Domaine De Monderlay	Por. Ch. Port Tiffany Du Domaine De Monderlay	Mr Mansuet	Mrs A. Fisher	16.10.86
Chantmarles Chivalry	D	Ch. Chantmarles Best Intentions	Ch. Chantmarles Proper Madam	Mrs M. Hayes	Mrs M. Hayes	7.9.86
Coletts Gold Sovereign	D	Coletts Creation	Ch. Coletts Charmaine	Mrs M. Coles	Mrs M. Coles	26.6.85
Beautara Height of Fashion	B	Verolian Emperor	Beautara Yours Truly	Mrs P. Green	Mrs P. Green	13.12.87
Verolian Al Pacino	D	Ch. Ozmilion Dedication	Ch. Verolian the Adventuress	Mrs V. Sameja-Hilliard	Mrs V. Sameja-Hilliard	16.10.87
Chantmarles Gaiety	B	Ch. Chantmarles Chivalry	Chantmarles Audacity	Mrs M. Hayes	Mrs M. Hayes	6.12.87
Cyndahl Royal Celebrity	D	Bradstara Royalist	Chelsea Girl of Cyndahl	Mrs E. Morris	Mrs E. Morris	3.8.84
Chevawn Special Engagement	D	Chevawn Special Charmer	Sharisa Missys Madam	Mrs J. Campion	Mrs W. White	1.8.86

Name of Champion	Sex	Sire	Dam	Breeder	Owner	Date of Birth
1990						
Ozmilion Infatuation	D	Ch. and Ir. Ch. Ozmilion Sensation	Ch. Ozmilion Hopelessly In Love	Mr O.A. Sameja	Mr O.A. Sameja	24.6.88
Ozmilion Irresistable Love	B	Ch. and Ir. Ch. Ozmilion Sensation	Ch. Ozmilion Hearts Desire	Mr O.A. Sameja	Mr O.A. Sameja	1.11.88
Ozmilion Aspect of Love	B	Ch. and Ir. Ch. Ozmilion Sensation	Ch. Ozmilion Dance of Romance	Mr O.A. Sameja	Mr O.A. Sameja	4.1.89
Pittens Dimple Twinkle	B	Coppersfield Whisky Mac	Geradene Twinkle Star	Mrs H. Ridgewell	Mrs H. Ridgewell	3.5.87
Beautara Some Charmer	B	Verolian Emperor	Beautara Yours Truly	Mrs P. Green	Mrs P. Green	13.12.87
Davonnes Replica	D	Ch. Royalties Reflex	Davonnes Golden Delight	Mrs Y. Windsor	Mrs Y. Windsor	31.7.86
Clantalon Credentials	D	Ch. Clantalon Contention	Clantalon Charisma	Mr & Mrs D. McKay	Mr & Mrs D. McKay	27.6.88
Typros New Generation	B	Ch. Ozmilion Admiration	Macstroud's First Choice	Mrs G. Da Silva	Mrs G. Da Silva	22.1.88

Glossary

Affix   Affixes are usually attached to dogs' registered names in order to identify them with particular kennels.

Almond eye   The shape of the eye opening, which slants upwards at the outer edge, thus giving it an almond shape.

Apple head   A domed skull.

Bat ear   An erect ear, broad at base, rounded or semi-circular at top with ear opening directly in front.

BOB   Best of Breed. A dog who has beaten all others of his breed.

Beard   Hair that grows around and under the lower jaw.

Bitch   A female dog.

Bloom   Glossiness of coat.

Brace   Two dogs exhibited together.

Brisket   That part of the body in front of the chest and between the forelegs.

BIS   Best in Show or Best of Sex. A dog who has beaten all others or all others of his sex relatively.

Brood-bitch   A female used for breeding.

Butterfly nose   When the nostrils show flesh colour interspersed with the black pigment.

Button ears   Ears which drop over in front covering the opening of the ear.

Canines   The four large teeth in the front of the mouth.

Cat ears   Very small V-shaped ears carried erect.

Cat feet   Short, round and deep feet, said to resemble those of a cat.

CC   Challenge Certificate. A Kennel Club award given by a judge for the best dog of his or her sex in a breed at a Championship show.

Champion (Ch.)   The holder of three CCs awarded by three different judges.

Character   A combination of the essential points of appearance said to be typical of the breed.

Cloddy   Thick-set build or plodding dog.

Close coupled   Short in length between the shoulders and the hip-bones.

Cobby   Compact, short-bodied.

Condition   Refers to the general appearance of the dog with regard to health, coat and demeanour.

Conformation   The form and structure of the bone of the dog in comparison with the requirements of the Breed Standard.

Corky   Active, alert dog.

Couplings   Body between the withers and the hip-bones.

Cow-hocked   When the hocks are bent inwards.

Crest   The arched portion of the back of the neck.

Cropping   The cutting of the ear leather to get the ear to stand erect.

Crossbred   A dog whose sire and dam are of two different breeds.

Crown   The highest part of the head.

Cryptorchid   Male dog with neither testical visible.

Dam   The female parent of puppies.

Dew-claws   Extra claws on the inside of front and/or back legs, which are better removed a few days after birth.

Dewlap   Loose skin under the throat.

Domed skull   Also called apple head – a fault in the Yorkshire Terrier.

Dock   To shorten the tail by cutting.

Dudley nose   Flesh-coloured or light-brown nostrils – a bad fault in the Yorkshire Terrier.

Expression   A combination of the colour, size and placement of the eyes and ears to give the typical expression associated with the breed.

Fall   The shape of the head which commences at the back of the skull to the end of the muzzle.

Feathering   Longer hair fringe on ears, legs, tail or body.

Flank   The side of the body between the last rib and the hip.

Flat sided   Ribs insufficiently rounded as they meet the breastbone.

Flop ears   Broad ears which fall to the sides of the head.

Fly ears   Semi-erect ears which stand out from the side of the head.

Front All that can be seen from the front but having special reference to the soundness of the brisket and the forelegs.

Gay Tail Tail which is carried above the top line.

Gestation The period during which a bitch carries her young – normally sixty-three days.

Good doer A dog who does well without any special treatment and has thrived from birth.

Hare foot A narrow foot.

Heat A bitch is said to be on or in heat during the period when she is in season (oestrus).

Height Vertical measurement from the ground to the top of the shoulders.

Hocks The joints in the hind legs between the pasterns and the stifles.

In-breeding The planned mating of related dogs in order to perpetuate certain characteristics which are desirable.

International Champion (Int. Ch.) A dog who has been awarded Championship status in more than one country.

Leather The skin of the ear flap.

Leather ears Without hair, usually lost through a form of mange.

Level bite The front of the upper and lower jaws meeting exactly.

Loin That part of the body between the last rib and the hindquarters.

Lumber Excess fat on a dog.

Lumbering Clumsy in action with awkward gait.

Maiden   An unmated bitch.

Monorchid   A male dog having only one testicle apparent.

Muzzle   The head in front of the eyes, combining nose and jaws.

Olfactory   Pertaining to the sense of smell.

Out at elbows   Having the elbow joints noticeably turned away from the body.

Out at shoulders   Shoulder blades set in such a way that the joints are too wide, and jut out from the body.

Outcrossing   The mating of unrelated dogs of the same breed.

Overshot   Having the upper incisors overlapping in the front teeth of the lower jaw.

Pad   The soles of the feet.

Pastern   The lower part of the leg below the hock on the hind leg and below the knee on the foreleg.

Pincer bite   A bite where the incisor teeth meet exactly.

Points   Colour on face, ears, legs and tail in contrast to the rest of the body colour.

Prick ear   Ear carried erect and pointed at tip.

Roach back   Upward curvature of back – poor top line. A bad fault in a Yorkshire Terrier.

Scapula   The shoulder blade.

Scissor bite   A bite in which the upper teeth just barely overlap the lower teeth.

Septum   The vertical dividing line between the two nostrils.

Slab sides   Insufficient spring of ribs.

Snipy   When the dogs muzzle is too long and narrow.

Sooty   Dark hair in the tan. This is a very bad fault in a Yorkshire Terrier.

Splay feet   The toes are spread wide apart.

Spring of rib   The degree of rib roundness.

Staring coat   Dry harsh hair.

Sternum   Breastbone.

Stop   The depression between and immediately in front of the eyes.

Sway back   A back that instead of being straight between withers and hip-line, curves downwards.

Topknot   Tuft of hair on top of head.

Type   The distinguishing characteristics essential to a dog to measure his worth against the Breed Standard.

Undershot   Having the lower incisors projecting beyond the upper jaw when the mouth is closed.

Weedy   Lacking in substance and too light in bone.

Wheel back   Roach back.

Withers   The highest part of the body just behind the neck.

Appendix 1

Old UK Breed Standard

General appearance should be that of a long coated toy terrier, the coat hanging quite straight and evenly down each side, a parting extending from the nose to the end of the tail.

The animal should be very compact and neat, the carriage being very upright and having an important air. The general outline should convey the existence of a vigorous and well-proportioned body.

Head

Should be rather small and flat, not too prominent or round in the skull, nor too long in the muzzle, with a perfect black nose. The fall on the head to be long, of rich golden tan, deep in colour at the sides of the head about the ear roots, and on the muzzle where it should be very long. The hair on the chest a rich bright tan. On no account must the tan on the head extend to the neck nor must there be any sooty or dark hair intermingled with any of the tan.

Eyes

Medium dark and sparkling, having a sharp intelligent expression and placed so as to look directly forward. They should not be prominent and the edge of the eyelids should be of a dark colour.

Ears

Small V-shaped and carried erect and not far apart, covered with short hair, colour to be of a deep rich tan.

Mouth

Perfectly even, with teeth as sound as possible. An animal having lost any teeth through accident not a fault providing the jaws are even.

Body

Very compact and good loin. Level on the top of the back.

Forequarters

Legs quite straight, well covered with hair of rich golden tan a few shades lighter at the ends than at the roots, not extending higher on the forelegs than the elbow.

Hindquarters

Legs quite straight, well covered with hair of rich golden tan a few shades lighter at the ends than at the roots, not extending higher on the hind legs than the stifle.

Coat

The hair on the body moderately long and perfectly straight (not wavy), glossy, like silk and of fine texture.

Colour

A dark steel blue (not silver blue) extending from the occiput (or back of skull) to the root of tail, and on no account mingled with fawn, bronze or dark hairs. The hair on the chest a bright rich tan. All hair should be darker at the roots than in the middle, shading to a still brighter tan at the tips.

Weight and Size

Weight up to seven pounds.

Appendix 2

Useful Addresses

Yorkshire Terrier Clubs in the UK

Cheshire and North Wales Yorkshire Terrier Society
Mrs J. Bebbington
70 Middlewich St
Cheshire
CW4 4DG

Eastern Counties Yorkshire Terrier Club
Mrs E. Bardwell
Orchard House
The Street
Dalham
Nr Newmarket
Suffolk CB8 8TH

Lincoln and Humberside Yorkshire Terrier Club
Mr B.R. Lees
109 Nightingale Crescent
Birchwood
Lincoln LN6 0JR

Midland Yorkshire Terrier Club
Mrs S. Taylor
47 Bankside Crescent
Streetly
Sutton Coldfield
West Midlands
B74 2HZ

Northern Counties Yorkshire Terrier Club
Mr P. Bursnoll
2 Manor Road
Shevington
Wigan
Lancashire WV6 8EE

South-Western Yorkshire Terrier Club
Mrs I. Millard
6 St Andrews Road
Backwell
Bristol
BS19 3DL

Ulster Yorkshire Terrier Club
Mrs M. Lamont
65 Old Dundonald Road
Belfast
BT16 0XS

The Yorkshire Terrier Club
Mrs P. Osborne
Polliam
19 Avebury Avenue
Ramsgate
Kent CT11 8BB

Yorkshire Terrier Club of Scotland
Mrs I. Rae
51 Calder Grove
Sighthill
Edinburgh
EH11 4NB

Yorkshire Terrier Club of South Wales
Mr T.M. Evans
14 Stuart Street
Treorchy
Rhondda
Mid Glamorgan
CF42 6SN

National Kennel Clubs

Australia
Australian National Kennel Council
Royal Show Ground
Ascot Vale
Victoria

Belgium
Société Royale Saint-Hubert
Avenue de l'Armée 25
B–1040 Brussels

Canada
Canadian Kennel Club
111 Eglinton Avenue
East Toronto 12

FCI
Fédération Cynologique Internationale
Rue Leopold 11
14 B-6530 Turin
Belgium

France
Société Centrale Canine
215 Rue St. Denis
75083 Paris
Cedex 20

Germany
Verbund für das Deutsche Hundewesen (VDH)
Schwanenstrasse 30
Dortmund

Holland
Raad van Beheer op Gebied in Netherland
Emmalaan 16
Amsterdam

Hong Kong
Hong Kong Kennel Club
3rd Floor
28B Stanley Street
Hong Kong

Ireland
Irish Kennel Club
23 Earlsfort Terrace
Dublin 2

Italy
Ente Nazionale Della Cinofilia Italiana
Viale Premuda
21 Milan

Malaysia
Malaysian Kennel Association
PO Box 559
Kuala Lumpur
Malaya

Sweden
Svenska Kennelklubben
Luntmakagaten 40
Box 1308
1183 Stockholm

UK
The Kennel Club
1/4 Clarges Street
Piccadilly
London

USA
American Kennel Club
51 Madison Avenue
New York
NY1010

The above kennel clubs will be able to supply you with a list of Yorkshire Terrier clubs within their countries.

Bibliography

Dangerfield, Stanley   *The International Encyclopaedia of Dogs*, Pelham Books Ltd

Harmar, H.   *Showing Dogs*, John Gifford Ltd

Huxam, Mona   *All About the Yorkshire Terrier*, Pelham Books Ltd (1971)

Noted Authors   *Jones's Animal Nursing*, Pergamon Press Ltd

Munday, Ethel   *The Yorkshire Terrier*, Popular Dogs Publishing Co. (1958)

Ransome, Jackie   *A Petlove Guide to Yorkshire Terriers*, Salamander Books (1988)

Swan, Annie   *The Yorkshire Terrier*, Nicholson & Watson (1958)

White, Kay   *Dogs: Their Mating, Whelping and Weaning*, K & R Books Ltd

Whitehead, Hector F.   *The Yorkshire Terrier*, W & G Foyle Ltd (1961)

The reader is recommended to subscribe to one of the national dog journals if they wish to keep abreast of all developments and news on their breed. The addresses of the various journals are available from your national kennel club.

Index

(Page numbers in italics refer to illustrations.)